HIDDEN TREASURES

PLYMOUTH

Edited by Steve Twelvetree

First published in Great Britain in 2002 by
YOUNG WRITERS
Remus House,
Coltsfoot Drive,
Peterborough, PE2 9JX
Telephone (01733) 890066

HB ISBN 0 75433 794 4
SB ISBN 0 75433 795 2

FOREWORD

This year, the Young Writers' Hidden Treasures competition proudly presents a showcase of the best poetic talent from over 72,000 up-and-coming writers nationwide.

Young Writers was established in 1991 and we are still successful, even in today's technologically-led world, in promoting and encouraging the reading and writing of poetry.

The thought, effort, imagination and hard work put into each poem impressed us all, and once again, the task of selecting poems was a difficult one, but nevertheless, an enjoyable experience.

We hope you are as pleased as we are with the final selection and that you and your family continue to be entertained with *Hidden Treasures Plymouth* for many years to come.

CONTENTS

Jason Lam	65
Emily Bowden	65
Lisa Congdon	66
Kirstin Dunn	66
Catherine Casey	66
Jamie-Lee Crockett	67
Jake Cooper	67
Charlotte Jackson	68
Cody Marley	68
Beth Dymond	69
Joe Shill	69
Jasmine Lawry-Lovidge	70
Laura Edyveane	70
Christopher Stribley	71
Jack Broadhurst	71
Nicholas Sinnett	72
Reanne Letts	72

High Street Primary School

Matthew King, Michael Martin & Geordie White	73
Josie Dunne	73
Christopher Pinn	74

Hyde Park Junior School

Syeda Kobir	74
Oliver Burton	75
Adam Oats	75
Bethany Rogers	76
Josh Bunch	76
Connie Watson	77
Lauren Clark	77
Ella Kenny	78
Lauren Phillips	78
Michael Warran	78
Francesca Green	79
Oscar Mo	79
Samuel Burgess	80

Thomas Stenhouse-Pyne	80
Connor Legg	81

Langley Junior School

Ben Robins	81
Bethany Jagger	82
Layla Ahmadi	82
Carly Johnson	83
Annie Ingram	83
Sarah Hill	84
Lauren Hall	84
Sophie Donovan	85
Emily Laverick	86
Louise Elford	87
Kathryn Langston	88
Robyn Lunt	88
Caroline Clark	89
Anna Rashleigh	90
Stephanie Pearce	91

Montpelier Junior School

Kerry Shilson	91
Caroline George	92
Louise Stewart	92
Chelsey Lindup	93
Melissa Curtis	94
Mark Wilson	95
Edward Privett	96
Leanne Earnshaw	96
Nathan Biship	97
Elliot Hugh	97
Philippa Starr	98
Grant Kennedy	98
Katie Wall	99
Nicola Gill	99
Laura Browne	100
Jodie Davey	100
Elisha Searl	101

The Poems

HOME FROM SCHOOL

Hearing the cooking
Loudly blaring in the kitchen.
Hearing my mum chattering
Quietly on the phone.
Hearing my brother frantically
Playing on his PlayStation.
Seeing my rabbit speeding after my cat.
Seeing my new, golden lounge wallpaper
Like gleaming gold.
Seeing my new, bright, fresh flowers
In my bright pink room.
Seeing my new silky, soft teddy
In my room.
Touching my lovely hot radiator,
Right next to my door.
Smelling my lovely hot stew,
Sizzling on the boiling hot oven rings.
Tasting my chocolate from
My box of Carnations.
Seeing my silky, soft cat
As she prances up on to my lap.
Tasting my new bun set
Which tastes like toffee.
Sniffing the whiff of my mum
Cooking fish for tea.
Gazing at the rain outside my window,
Behind my blinds.
Staring at my ceiling as
I am lying on my bed.
Looking at my swing swinging
Automatically in the wind.
Staring at my fish
As I am going up my stairs.

Sophie Rowe (8)
Boringdon Primary School

BACK FROM SCHOOL

Smelling freshly-baked steak pie
Just coming out of the oven,
Smelling the aroma of crunchy rock cakes,
Just put on the rack by my mum,
Smelling the crumpets under the grill,
Sizzling softly,
Smelling a roast chicken, covered in spicy gravy
With carrots, peas, cauliflower and broccoli,
All in one bowl.
Smelling the chocolate being melted
For profiteroles,
Hearing the booming of the news on the TV
About a volcano erupting and a huge lava flow.
Hearing my next door's cat purring
In the back garden,
Hearing my friend's dog,
Squealing like a dolphin,
Hearing my cousin's PlayStation,
As if my ears were next to a train's engine.
Hearing the pitter-patter from the rain
Suddenly turn into a flood.

Heather Foulkes (8)
Boringdon Primary School

AT HOME

Seeing my gigantic mirror with a gold frame,
Seeing my toys stacked away neatly,
Seeing my next-door neighbour asking to play,
Seeing my dad frying my big, fat, juicy sausage,
Feeling my enchanting hazel-brown, patch dog
Licking my hand softly,
Feeling my level, transparent glass of Sunny Delight,
Feeling the plastic, tapping keys of the computer.

Hearing the TV playing quietly,
Hearing cars zooming down the street,
Like being on the motorway,
Hearing my dog crunching her bone, deafeningly,
Hearing my sister sounding like a stampede
Of elephants running down the stairs,
Hearing my stereo being played by my friends.

Rebecca Hendra (9)
Boringdon Primary School

A POEM OF SENSES

Touching the bumpy TV remote and pointing it
At the dusky black, cuboid-faced TV.
Touching my silky smooth school shoes
The second I walk through the door.
Touching the kind of bumpy PlayStation
Controller with lots of vibration.
Touching the sticky Sellotape that sticks
To my fingers and never comes off them.
Touching the fluffy home clothes that go over my head
And on my blazing hot body, like a sweltering hot fire.

Hearing the builders banging as raucous as
An aeroplane shooting through the air at 500mph.
Hearing the TV roaring as loud as it could be.
Hearing the washing machine spinning as rapidly as possible.
Hearing my brother's hi-fi singing like a fullpitch monkey.
Hearing my tap dripping quietly, like a bush rustling.

Smelling the sweet tea cooking when I walk through the door,
Smelling the wet paint of the whitest wall,
Smelling the sawdust of the sharp chainsaw, like little millions.

Harry Smith (8)
Boringdon Primary School

MY FUTURE

What will be
Left here for me
When I grow up?

Will the blinding
Sunlight be blocked
By the ozone layer?

Will the roaring tigers
Still be used for
Their skins and medicines?

Will planet Earth be
The only remaining planet
With living people?

Could motorbikes still have
Two wheels, or could it
Change to four wheels?

Could we have brown
Water and will
It change our environment?

Oliver Folds (9)
Boringdon Primary School

THINGS ALL AROUND ME

Seeing a doormat, all rough, with
Stairs right in front of me, all zigzaggy.
Seeing balloons glistening in my front room.
Seeing candles all bright, like a light.
Seeing towels, dull and dusky pink.
Seeing wood flooring that makes your feet freeze.

Hearing clocks ticking in the front room.
Hearing cats screeching in my back garden,
Hearing the dripping of the taps in my bathroom.
Hearing my next door's little boy,
Screaming and shouting like an ill monkey.
Hearing children playing on my street.

Danielle Barnes (9)
Boringdon Primary School

MY FUTURE

What will be
Left here for me
When I grow up?

Will rivers still flow?
Will the blue water
Still be clean?

Will the fields still be green?
Will plants still be able to grow,
Or will they be destroyed?

Will the foxes still be alive,
Or will they be destroyed
By the humans in the forest?

Will people be able to visit planets
And breathe pure air up there too,
Or will there be no goodness?

Will green leaves still be on the trees
And still change colour,
Or will they come falling down?

Danielle Charles (8)
Boringdon Primary School

HOME SENSES

Hearing noisy gossip
In the small front room.
Hearing the box-like TV
Blaring at me.
Hearing the wind
Whistling outside.
Hearing my little sisters,
Chatting loudly.

Touching my clear, white
Rabbit-like velvet.
Touching my soft and rough sofa.
Touching my soaked, soggy shoes which
Have just been out in the pouring rain.
Touching my slippery cup
Just lifted out of my bag.

Seeing the gentle cat
Slouching on the sofa.
Seeing my bumpy stairs,
Like a slimy snake.
Seeing my cuboid kitchen,
Ready to be cooked in.
Seeing my granny doing
The hard ironing.

Sophie Wallis (8)
Boringdon Primary School

SENSES AT HOME

Hearing children striding home from school,
Sounding like monkeys in a cage.
Hearing Connor's gorgeous porch
Being built by Bob the Builder.
Hearing the crashing nails into the hard wood
Like a woodpecker pecking at a tree.
Hearing Connor's mum having a conversation,
Moaning about the builder.
Hearing my mum slamming cupboards and drawers upstairs,
Like a bomb hitting the Earth.
Hearing a crow squawking in a high pitch,
Holding tightly onto a branch.
Hearing sausages sizzling in a pan for my tea,
With all the fat bubbling.
Tasting delicious chocolate melting in my mouth,
Like a microwave in my mouth melting it.
Tasting a cup of tea in my mouth
Is like a needed drink for a thirsty man.
Tasting my grandma's gorgeous soup at teatime,
Like it was so good, she could go on Ready Steady Cook.
Touching the squashy TV remote and
Flicking through all the channels to see what's on.
Touching my sister's skipping rope and
Playing with it in the living room.

Sam Bennell (8)
Boringdon Primary School

HOME FROM SCHOOL

Hearing sausages sizzling in the plentiful wok
Makes my tummy tingle!
Hearing my mum's bombastic music is like
Listening to a monkey screeching at full pitch!
Hearing my grandad crackling the
Skinny sheets of his newspaper.
Hearing the horrendously loud neighbours
Clattering around next door!
Smelling the freshly cooked aroma of newly-baked bread
Wafting through the hall like fresh berries.
Smelling the hair-raising smell of my mum's Chanel No5
Drifting through the air.
Smelling my grandad's fountain pen ink
As he writes with it.

Jessica Howard (9)
Boringdon Primary School

COMING HOME

Hearing my pretty sister on the computer, tapping noisily,
Hearing my mum putting big sausages in the big deep fat fryer,
Hearing my dad banging on the wall,
Hearing my sister's music like a volcano exploding.

Seeing the big, blue, comfortable sofa
In the large, blue dining room.
Seeing my dad frying fishy bits in a wok.

Feeling my mum's big glass of cold cider in a circular cup,
Feeling the black buttons on the big controller.

Amy Burton (9)
Boringdon Primary School

WHEN I COME IN FROM SCHOOL

Seeing my furry cat lying about in the strong breeze.
Seeing my rats rattling their cage on top
Of my large, high, snake tank.
Seeing my scaly snake sliding in his warm, hot tank.
Hearing my dinner boiling in the huge, hot oven.
Hearing the radio squealing as my dad turns it to maximum.
Hearing my drink being thrown out.
Smelling my sausages sizzling in a frying pan.
Smelling the oil off the large pan.
Smelling the dinner being dished onto my plate.
Tasting my dinner when it hits my tongue.
Tasting the sausages hitting my tongue,
Which is as wet as the rain.
Eating the sandwich that my mum prepares for me on a Tuesday.
Touching my homework book, like a field that hasn't been ploughed.
Touching the ladder on the end of my bed, like a big block of metal.
Touching the glass window, like a glass being melted.

Samuel Pinhey (9)
Boringdon Primary School

MY SENSES

Hearing the tasty chips in the oven sizzling.
Hearing my cat Sparky crunching and munching
                                    on his cat food.
Hearing my sisters booming on the piano.
Hearing the footsteps of somebody
Coming down the staircase.
Hearing the worker banging on the wall
With his old hammer.
Seeing my little sister, Naomi,
Bouncing on the couch like a chimpanzee.

Abigail Jones (8)
Boringdon Primary School

HOME FROM SCHOOL

Seeing my mum cooking a meal in the kitchen.
Seeing my little sister run and turn on the television,
Seeing my little sister sink into the massive sofa
As she gazes at the reflection.
Seeing Dad whizz past on his shiny motorbike.
Seeing Mum also sink into the sofa
And fall into a deep gaze.

Hearing the TV bellow at my sister
Like a big herd of elephants.
Hearing my mum shout at me like a bellow.
Hearing a ring at the doorbell
Like someone playing saucepans.
Hearing birds sing like a piano at full pitch.
Hearing my dad's bike zoom past
Like an ostrich.
Hearing my cat scratch agonisingly at the sofa,
Like a monkey in a zoo.

Touching the soft cat and its silky hair.
Touching the remote control and
Its hard and bumpy buttons.
Touching the sofa's warm arms as I relax.

Thomas Sansford (8)
Boringdon Primary School

HOME POEM

Eating crunchy, crispy snacks.
Eating ten chocolates.
Eating my sizzling sausages, frying in the pan.

Eating my tasty sweets from Christmas.
Touching the tip of my pen.
Touching the soft keys of my gigantic computer.

Dominic Young (9)
Boringdon Primary School

HOME FROM SCHOOL

Hearing my terrible sisters stomp loudly,
Like noisy elephants.
Hearing the chips sizzling loudly in the pan.
Hearing my cat chomp on her vegetables, greedily.
Hearing Mum bawl at the terrible girls
And send them to their rooms.
Hearing the rain speed down loudly on the roof.
Hearing the fire engine zoom past at full speed.
Hearing the stereo booming away at full volume.
Hearing my sister sing like a chattering monkey.
Hearing the booming noise of the computer.
Hearing the gigantic fridge hum a low hum.
Seeing the toys scattered over the room like a massive tip.
Seeing my sister cry like a baby.
Seeing my dad chase the girls like an angry bull.
Seeing my bed messy like a wreck.
Seeing the sausages sizzling in the pan.
Seeing my toy tower exploded into bits.
Seeing the wind ram against the trees.
Seeing my sister focus on the TV.
Seeing my mum smack the girls.
Seeing my toy animals lying on my bed.
Seeing a truck whizz by at 65mph.

Timothy Landricombe (9)
Boringdon Primary School

MY FUTURE

What will be
Left for me
When I grow up?

Will there be fruit
For people to eat
When they want it?

Will there be water
For people to drink
And to survive?

Will there be minibuses
For over-aged people
To travel?

Will there be
Fresh sea for people
To swim in?

Will there be sunlight
For people to go out
To play with their best mates?

Jamie Ramsay (9)
Boringdon Primary School

HOME TIME

Smelling the fresh aroma of ham and chicken pie,
Flowing out of the thin, crispy pastry.
Smelling thick bacon hissing and sizzling
In the sooty black pan.
Smelling the wonderful aroma of pesto
Slipping around the large bowl.
Smelling the hot, wavy chips frying,
Nearly ready to taste.

Hearing the puffing and rumbling noise of
The huge tractor storming up the hill.
Hearing my brother's music and ear-splitting
Booming out of his bedroom.
Listening to my gerbil gnawing and nibbling
At her wooden chew toys.
Hearing four plump sausages
Popping and crackling in the pan.
Hearing the whirling sound of my giant tree
Swaying in the silent breeze.

Paige Sim (9)
Boringdon Primary School

MY FUTURE

What will be
Left here for me
When I grow up?

Will bees still exist
To drink the pollen
From flowers?

What will be left of trees,
Green and brown trees,
Will their trunks be firm and hard?

Will blue rivers
Be destroyed and poisoned
By factories' construction?

Will the world still exist,
With its round, sphere shape,
With its quick spin?

Lewis Rawlings (8)
Boringdon Primary School

IN MY HOUSE

Touching my mum's fluffy rabbits hopping happily round the garden.
Touching my plump, fuzzy rat, scuttling round his cage.
Touching our plastic remote control to turn on the TV.
Touching my slippery CD cases with shiny CDs inside them.
Touching my small, orange teddy bear,
Like lying on a pile of snow-white feathers.
Touching a smooth, shiny chocolate wrapper,
Like touching the finest silk.

Seeing my horrible, annoying brother dressing like a dizzy monkey
Trying to put shorts on his head.
Seeing my sympathetic mum cooking up a tasty tea.
Seeing roaring cars zooming down my busy street.
Seeing my terrorising brother's room like a rabbit hutch!
Seeing rows of interesting books along my bookshelf.

Hearing my booming music blasting out from my CD player.
Hearing my little brother squealing loudly when Dad tickles him,
Like a lamb baaing at full volume.
Hearing my dad's deafening motorbike as he races off to his
                                                friend's house.
Hearing the huge microwave buzzing loudly,
Like a hundred bees buzzing in your ear.

Elizabeth Tobin (8)
Boringdon Primary School

CROSS WAY SENSES

Hearing the booming sound of the black, dusty TV
                                in the dining room.
Hearing the crispy chips in the black, rusty pan.
Hearing the rumbling noise of the white tumble-drier.
Hearing the water splashing about in the white kettle.

Touching the blue cup that slips out of my hand and
Onto the cold cream tiles.
Touching a smooth, white, bumpy Polo.
Touching the cold, pale blue handle of the freezing cold fridge.
Touching a rough black shoe with long, muddy laces.

Jessica McGlinchey (9)
Boringdon Primary School

MY SENSES

Seeing my midnight-black dog running like a panther,
Up and down the hallway frantically.
Seeing my brother staring at the warm, light glow
Of the computer screen, like daylight.
Seeing my mum set the table with our sparkly silver dinner set,
Like crystals for dinner.
Seeing my gloomy cat sleeping in his slippery basket,
His bedding like oily seal's skin.
Seeing the cars zoom past our house
Like leopards chasing buffalo.

Hearing my midnight-black dog barking at the neighbours
Like a pack of exulting hyenas.
Hearing my sister's bombastic music downstairs.
Hearing my gloomy cat blaring like
An antelope warning a tiger.
Hearing the whistling through the window.

Tasting my mum's hot and spicy, gorgeous curry
Like a blazing fire.
Tasting my ice cream trickling down my throat
Like a stream of sticky toffee.
Tasting my sweet Mars Bar melting in my throat.

Matthew Davies (8)
Boringdon Primary School

MY FUTURE

What will be
Left here for me
When I grow up?

Will cows be healthy
And safe to eat,
And give us all the goodness?

What will the sea
Be like when it's clean?
Will a ship sail across?

What will cars be like?
Will they be fast or slow?
They might fly or not fly!

Will fields still be green,
Or will tarmac cover
On top of them?

Will plants still grow?
Will trees uproot because
Bulldozers build roads?

Hollie Perks (9)
Boringdon Primary School

HOME SENSES

Hearing my sleek cat softly purring by the roasting fire,
Hearing the stairs crackling as my deafening brother
                                        stomps up the stairs.
Hearing the sound of the booming television
As I sit in the cosy couch.

Charlotte Bromley (8)
Boringdon Primary School

AT HOME

Hearing a squeaky alarm go on
As I walk through the door.
Hearing the Velcro on my itchy book bag
As I open the top.
Hearing myself running up the squeaky stairs.
Hearing a fast, loud, 'ting' as I
Get into my cold, dusty room.
Hearing myself running down the straight
Then curved stairs.
Hearing the melted cheese
Bubbling on my dinner.
Feeling the itchy book bag
As I open the top.
Feeling a plastic, rubbery part of my book bag
As I put my hand inside.

Aimie Baker (8)
Boringdon Primary School

AT HOME

Watching my kitten curled up on my lap.
Seeing the stairs go up so straight,
Then suddenly curve round to a halt.
Seeing the fire blaze and hiss and repeat.
Seeing the coffee table shake when I sit on it,
Then quiver when my cat leaps onto me.
Gazing at my reflection in the shining,
Tall mirror at the end of my hall.
Watching the TV scream at me while I do homework.

Naomi Skentelbery (9)
Boringdon Primary School

SENSES AT HOME

Stroking my dog's gorgeous, golden, woolly fur
As soon as I collapse in the door.
She runs and runs and runs,
Whizzing up the blue stairs, pouncing and sliding
All over our beech-coloured, laminated flooring
And springs up on to my knees.

Touching my smooth, bumpy wallpaper,
Like gnawed tree bark.
Touching the cold, slippery pine table
As I move it next to the computer.
Feeling the warm, rubbery game's packet
As I take out my favourite game.
Touching the smooth, hard PC keyboard
As I go to play the game.

Smelling the roast chicken in the oven,
Nearly ready to come out.
Smelling Mum's home-made bread in the bread maker
Makes my tummy sound like an earthquake.

Hearing the awful, noisy radio yelling at me
And the TV screeching at me.
Hearing my mum talking to my dad about what
The weather is going to be like the next day.
Hearing my brother trotting around upstairs
Like a volcano exploding.

Melanie Baldock (9)
Boringdon Primary School

HOME FROM SCHOOL

Hearing my sister Rachel fluently reading
Her favourite book to Mum.
Hearing the television blaring loudly at me
From the cosy living room, making my ears tingle.
Hearing the telephone ringing sharply,
Like a non-stop, high-pitched bleep.
Hearing the birds chirping joyfully
In the high, green trees.
Hearing the distant noises of sawing and drilling
As my dad works hard in the chilly garage.
Hearing my sister's deafening music booming
Through the house like listening to a group of
Non-stop, full-volume singing monkeys.

Seeing children skipping and running home from school,
Like they have no cares in the world.
Seeing my house, which is familiar and safe.
Seeing the Chuckle Brothers on the television,
Acting like a pair of crazy lunatics.
Seeing a light like a dazzling star.
Seeing cars whizzing past like swift rockets.

Tasting sweet, delicious chocolate
That melts in my mouth.
Tasting sizzling, meaty steak with
Salty, hot chips.
Tasting cool apple juice that is
Fruity and fresh.

Hannah Moran (9)
Boringdon Primary School

HOME FROM SCHOOL

Seeing my towering dad chatting on the little telephone
With rubbery jet-black and white buttons.
Seeing my plastic remote control with scarlet red buttons.
Seeing my noisy bird chirping loudly sitting on his wooden perch.
Seeing the massive television blaring through the house
Like a bear growling at full pitch.

Touching the freezing kitchen floor, like stepping on to the Antarctic.
Touching my sofa, like leaping on a waterbed.
Touching the white radiator that is hot, like a bit of boiling sand
from the desert.

Hearing my bird whistling like a referee blowing his whistle.
Hearing my brother yelling like a monkey in a bad mood.
Hearing the clock ticking slowly.

Kerry Loveys (9)
Boringdon Primary School

AFTER SCHOOL

Touching the wet, slimy door handle.
Touching my dog's wet fur.
Touching my dog's wet, slimy tongue on my face.
Touching my smelly shoes.
Touching my cold, slimy bag.
Touching the carpet with my smelly socks.
Touching my bag.
Touching my book bag.
Touching my smooth homework book.
Touching a hexagonal prism pencil.

Jonathan Perkins (8)
Boringdon Primary School

PEOPLE SENSES

Touching my scruffy hair,
all dropped down over my face.
Touching my shiny pink cup
that slips out of my hands.
Touching my remote control for my telly -
a small box of chocolates with lumps on the top.
Touching my slithery sofa
like a greasy snake.
Touching my crispy chocolate biscuit,
like a very thin pancake.

Seeing my lovely dad staring at the TV
like a monkey looking at his little baby chimp.
Seeing my furry stairs like a fluffy lion with a flat body.

Samantha Metters (8)
Boringdon Primary School

MY FUTURE

What will be
Here for me
When I grow up?

Will there be any
Eucalyptus leaves left
For koalas to eat?

Will pollution clog up
The Earth and the sea
And kill penguins?

Carl Brown (9)
Boringdon Primary School

MY FUTURE

What will be
Left here for me
When I grow up?

Will gorillas be extinct
In the future, or
Will they still be alive?

Will there be big,
Spaces, green fields
For us to play cricket on?

Will there be clean water
For us to swim in if
We keep throwing litter in?

Will there be clean water
For us to drink
From the rivers?

Sean Ward (8)
Boringdon Primary School

HOME AT LAST

Hearing the booming of the dusky television
In the front room with my little brother.
Hearing the round, clicking clock as
My heavy bag falls off my aching back.
Hearing the sizzling burgers in the oven.
Hearing my brother charging down the stairs
Like a stampede of elephants.

Seeing the steep stairs splitting into two narrow paths.
Seeing my hyper hamster thundering round in its ball
Like a car wheel going full blast.
Seeing my sparkling reflection in the glass.
Seeing my brother's soggy coat hanging off the
steaming radiator.

Connor Anderson (9)
Boringdon Primary School

MY FUTURE

What will be
Left for me
When I grow up?

Will the sea be clean
For the fish to swim
In the fresh and sparkling water?

Will the sun shine
To make the green
Grass grow?

Will the shops
Be open with
Lovely fresh food to eat?

Will we still
Have houses and
A bed to sleep in?

Will the planet be
Destroyed by
Our careless behaviour?

Jessica Read (9)
Boringdon Primary School

MY FUTURE

What will be
Left here for me
When I grow up?

Will the green, tall trees
In the forest
Still be high up in the sky?

Would the housing
Be destroyed by
Floods and tarmac?

How will blue,
Fresh water from
Rivers stay clean?

Could the wildlife survive
And the grass
Still be green?

Will the goodness
Still be in
Flowers and fruit?

Hannah Connolly (8)
Boringdon Primary School

MY FUTURE

What will be
Left here for me
When I grow up?

Where will tigers
Live if we cut
Down the jungle?

What will the dolphins
Eat if we poison
The water and kill the fish they eat?

Will there be any fresh vegetables
Left for us to eat if we
Destroy the ground?

Toni Perrin (8)
Boringdon Primary School

MY FUTURE

What will be
Left for me
When I grow up?

Will there be trees
For oxygen
For me?

Will air still be
Polluted from car fumes,
To breathe for animals and me?

Will wildlife die?
Will animals still survive?
Will water still be polluted for me to drink?

Will fruit and vegetables
Still be there, or will they rot
For people to eat?

Will people still hunt animals?
Will people give up hunting,
Or will they still hunt for me?

Douglas Miller (9)
Boringdon Primary School

MY FUTURE

What will be
Left here for me
When I grow up?

Will we be able
To design cars
That are able to fly?

Could an extinct
Animal come back to life,
Or will endangered species die?

Could you go on holiday
And go to the moon,
Or could you go on holiday in spaceships?

Will we still be
Able to eat healthy food
And fish and chips?

Will the air be
Polluted and have poison
In it, or will the air be pure?

When scientists discover
A new illness or disease,
Could they find a cure?

Helena Moore (9)
Boringdon Primary School

MY FUTURE

What will be
Left here for me
When I grow up?

Will rhinos still
Roam around to
Protect their skin?

Will I still be able
To walk through the dense forest
And hear the birds singing?

Will fields be green,
Or will they be
Covered in dirty tarmac?

Will we be able
To eat lovely chicken dinners,
Or will it make us ill?

Will the sea be clean
Enough to swim in,
Or will it be oily?

Will we still be able
To fly to different countries
On aeroplanes in safety?

Lisa Larcombe (8)
Boringdon Primary School

MY FUTURE

What will be
Left here for me
When I grow up?

What will have
Happened in the future?
Will there be different animals?

Will there be
Doctors or nurses
To look after our health?

Will there be buses
Or trains, or supersonic cars
For transport?

Will there be fizzy drinks,
Or will there just be
Fizzy, still drinks?

What happens when
The sea gets polluted?
Will the animals survive?

Will houses stay
Standing, or will
They just topple over?

Roseanne Burnman (8)
Boringdon Primary School

MY FUTURE

What will be
Left for me
When I grow up?

Will trees still be
Tall and green or
Won't there be any at all?

Will dogs still howl,
Will cats miaow,
Will plants and animals still survive?

Will the sea be
Blue or green,
Or will people poison the water?

Will seals still swim?
Will whales still sing?
Will sharks still attack?

Would we still drive in cars?
Will people drive motorbikes?
Will aeroplanes still fly?

Will air be all right
To breathe, or
Will people suffocate?

Danny Fowle (9)
Boringdon Primary School

MY FUTURE

What will be
Left here for me
When I grow up?

Where will tigers live
If their homes in Africa
Have been destroyed?

Will the sunlight
Affect our skin
And get us sunburnt?

What will be left
For transport
Instead of cars and vans?

Will fields still be green
And not be all
Brown and horrible?

What will be left
For fruits instead
Of normal fruits?

What will happen
To the sea in
Many years time?

Will there be
Rivers all blrown
Instead of blue?

Rachel Moran (9)
Boringdon Primary School

MY FUTURE

What will be
Left here for me
When I grow up?

Will blue fish swim,
While the sun is down,
In the deep, salty sea?

Will grey donkeys bray
And sit on the hay
In the clean, warm stable?

Where will grass grow,
If tarmac destroys the countryside,
While poison covers the Earth?

Will hunters takeover
And kill elephants
For their sharp tusks?

Will birds still fly,
While gliding through the sky,
Or will they die?

Will houses fall
As winds push by
And fall from the sky?

What will be
Left for me
When I grow up?

Emma Worth (8)
Boringdon Primary School

MY FUTURE

What will be
Left here for me
When I grow up?

Will people
Live on a
Different planet?

Could there be
No water or sea
For octopuses to swim in?

Would there be
Some new food
Or new games?

What would happen
If cows
Were extinct?

Could aliens
Take over
Our planet?

Adam Easterbrook (8)
Boringdon Primary School

MY FUTURE

What will be
Left for me
When I grow up?

Will hunters keep
Killing things
In the future?

Will blue whales
Still survive in
The water of pollution?

Would there be any
Green if we keep putting
Tarmac on the green?

Ben Hall (8)
Boringdon Primary School

MY FUTURE

What will be
Left here for me
When I grow up?

Will giraffes still eat
Green leaves from trees
In Africa?

Will we still
Have clean clothes
To wear?

Are we still
Going to have comfortable
Homes, or won't they exist?

Who will be
Our queen, who
Will rule the country?

Would we still
Have fresh air,
Like we have now?

Mitchell Tucker (9)
Boringdon Primary School

MY FUTURE

What will be
Left here for me
When I grow up?

Will giraffes still eat
Green leaves from
Trees in Africa?

Would meat still exist,
Or will people
Eat different food?

Are we still going to
Travel in cars,
Or will we have to walk?

When I grow up,
Will there be pure air to breathe,
Like these days?

Kerry Wrightson (8)
Boringdon Primary School

ALL SENSES

Feeling the control
For my silly brother's mini TV.

Touching the tiny tin of fish food.
Touching my big laptop and
Cardboard information CD cases.

Stroking the lead on my working pencil.
Touching the slippery, wooden floor,
Like an oiled slide.

Stephen Roberts (8)
Boringdon Primary School

MY FUTURE

What will be
Left here for me
When I grow up?

When I grow up,
Will there be any
Whales to sing in the sea?

When I grow up,
Will there be pure air
To breathe like today?

Will the sunlight
Still be bright,
Like a star?

Will the sea
Still be blue
And clean?

Will plants still
Be green,
Just like leaves?

Simon Dwyer (8)
Boringdon Primary School

MY BRANCHES

High in the branches of my tree,
You will not believe what I can see.
I can see all around, without my feet upon the ground.
The old horse in the field, the farmer out collecting his yield.
One day I went to see my tree, no longer was it there.
All that remained was a tree stump, bare.

Alexander Martin (10)
Brixton St Marys Primary School

I HAD A DREAM

I had a dream, I flew to the moon,
There were little people living there!
They made *me* queen of *their* land!

I wore a pink, frilly frock,
A glittery tiara and
A pink pair of dainty ballet slippers.

I sat upon a shiny, golden throne!
After I had a manicure,
I had a feast of my very own,
Then I floated through the air
Leading to a rose-petalled silk bed.

When I awoke, I found myself lying
On a tatty, cotton-covered quilt.
The only thing I couldn't explain
Was that next to me was the
Glittery tiara I had worn in my dream,
But it wasn't there the night before!
Could *you* explain?

Lyndsay Morris (11)
Brixton St Marys Primary School

MY DOG GEORGE

My dog has a cold, wet nose
And a tail that wags,
And he likes to lick me when I get home.
My dog's got a spot on his side.
When he sees me, he gives me a biscuit
So I can throw it for him.

Daniel Spry (9)
Brixton St Marys Primary School

LIGHTNING

I can make you hide
In shiver and dread,
So you'll run upstairs
And get tucked up in bed.

I am lightning.

I can light up the midnight sky,
Make fireworks weak.
But I am not weak,
And I never run away and squeak.

I am lightning.

Jack Springbett (10)
Brixton St Marys Primary School

A SMILE

When you frown,
Just turn it upside down
And you will have a smile.
When you feel mad,
Think of something glad,
There's no need to be sad,
Because God gave you a smile,
So keep it,
At least for a while.

Zoe Freeman (10)
Brixton St Marys Primary School

LOOKING AT OLD PHOTOS

Who's that? Aunty Mabel.
Who's that? Me, under the table.

Who's that? Uncle Billy.
Who's that? Me, being silly.

Who's that? Grandad Fred.
Who's that? Me, in bed.

Who's that? Grandma Joan.
Who's that? Me, throwing a stone.

Who's that? Brother Lee.
Who's that? Me, in a tree.

Who's that? My best friend.
Who's that? Me, going round the bend!

Olivia Harris (10)
Brixton St Marys Primary School

IT'S JUST MY PUSSY CAT

One night I woke up with a fright.
I walked down the stairs, frightened as a little mouse,
Forgetting I was in my own house, where it is safe.
I kept hearing tap, tap, tap.
Someone might be at the door, perhaps?
I walk up to the back door,
I open it, standing on the mat.
I am a silly girl, it's just my pussy cat.

Annette James (10)
Brixton St Marys Primary School

MY PONY ARNOLD

M ucking out, what a job,
Y ah-ha we go.

P erfectly loving,
O nly one Arnold.
N ight and day,
Y outhful he is.

A rnold, my pony,
R ugs, roughness and toughness,
N aughty and cheeky,
O nly 12.2 hands high.
L ove I give him,
D ennis the Menace springs to mind.

Lucy Daymond-McCowan (10)
Brixton St Marys Primary School

THE SLUG

I go as slow as I can go,
I leave trails in the snow.
I like warm areas,
I don't like big storms.
I live in a tree,
My heart is always full of glee.
I have three friends, Jeff, Shef and McBeth,
And what do you know?
My mum's name is Steff.

Jay Searle (10)
Brixton St Marys Primary School

My Family

My dad sits down snoozing lazily,
My sister is so crazy,
My mum's having a cup of tea,
I'm resting on Grandma's knees.

My auntie and uncle are drinking a pint,
My great-grandma is scared of heights.
The cat is walking across the ground,
The children are on the roundabout, spinning around.

My cousins are in the field,
They've got a shield.
My second cousins are inside,
They're doing some thing for a surprise.

Marianne Jarvis (10)
Brixton St Marys Primary School

My Brother And Me

I go to bed
And my brother bangs his head.
He wakes and opens the door.
My dad plays hardcore
And the neighbours bang on the door.
I go to turn the music down
And my dad was dressed like a clown
And my mum was in her nightgown.

Conor Daymond-McCowan (9)
Brixton St Marys Primary School

MY IMAGINARY FRIEND

I've an imaginary friend.
He says he's got a girlfriend.
He drives me up the wall,
He says he loves eating meatballs.
His name is Dean
And he hates to be clean.
He wants to go to school,
Because he thinks he'll be cool.
He's got dreadful hair
And a very stern glare,
But I don't really care,
Because he's always there.

Francesca Daniels (10)
Brixton St Marys Primary School

MY MUM

I love my mum,
She cooks great meals and
Helps me when I am stuck.
She is kind, caring and good luck.
She may get cross with me
And send me up to my room,
But I love her in the end.
She's not just any old mum.
She's my mum and I love her.

Elliott Lowe (10)
Brixton St Marys Primary School

SPRING COMES

Spring comes with a touch of frost,
Spring comes with green grass,
Spring comes with dazzling sun,
Spring comes with newborn animals,
Spring comes with less rain,
Spring comes with bright daffodils,
Spring ends with the start to summer.

Georgette Griffiths
Brixton St Marys Primary School

MY HAMSTER

My hamster, Quicksilver,
His coat is really shiny.
His claws are big, so are his paws.
At night he goes in his wheel,
Keeps us awake.
His teeth are big and
He bites and draws blood.
He is small, like a stone.

Craig Rattray (9)
Brixton St Marys Primary School

SUN

I am the sun,
I am very hot.
When you sunbathe,
You get hot.

You need a drink,
Crawl off the beach
Into the shade
Where I cannot reach you.

Stephen Clasby (9)
Brixton St Marys Primary School

WINTER

W inter is cold,
I   ce sheet beneath my feet,
N o sun,
T   oo cold to play,
E   very day is dark,
R apid rivers frozen.
     Winter is fun,
     I love winter.

Ellen Landricombe (10)
Brixton St Marys Primary School

MY PONY

My pony is good,
He loves carrots or apples,
He loves treats too.
He trots along the lanes,
Eh canters in fields,
He doesn't mind me putting on his tack,
He likes me leading him to his field.

Donna Ford (10)
Brixton St Marys Primary School

MY PET TORTOISE

My pet is really cool,
He makes me really mad,
Just like my dad,
But we are always friends
Because we are always together,
Forever and ever,
So it will always be fun.

Joshua Coggins (10)
Brixton St Marys Primary School

COLOURS

What is blue? The sea is blue,
With fishes swimming through.

What is green? A tree is green,
With birds in-between.

What is yellow? The sun is yellow,
All golden and mellow.

What is white? A swan is white,
With feathers very light.

What is grey? My road is grey,
Like a flat, long tray.

What is red? My pot is red,
It comes from the shed.

What is pink? My rose is pink,
Being watered in the sink.

Hannah Stamp (9)
Chaddlewood Junior School

WHEN THE WIND

When the wind is howling between the buildings,
It is a wolf, desperately searching for its lost cubs.
When the wind is whispering through the trees,
It is a bee, finding flowers for nectar.
When the wind is making a cold draught in the house,
It is a butterfly looking for a rose to sit upon.
When the wind is flickering flames in the fire,
It is a cunning fox jumping over the coal.
When the wind is blowing umbrellas inside out,
It is a lion ripping it apart and roaring.
When the wind is carrying a dandelion seed along,
It is a bird pecking at worms and taking seeds with him.
When the wind is breaking branches of a tree,
It is a monkey swinging from branch to branch.

Charlotte Espin (11)
Chaddlewood Junior School

SNOWING, SNOWING

Snowing, snowing all day long.
Footprints, dog prints, cat prints in the ground.
Looking, looking out of your window
Seeing all the children making snowmen,
Playing games, making angels in the snow.
People hiding, people sleighing down the hills.
Home time, home time, children moaning.
Bedtime, bedtime, children tiring.
Snug and cosy all tucked up in their beds,
Snowing, snowing.

Jessica Larkin (9)
Chaddlewood Junior School

THE SIEGE OF TROY

A silvery moon is reflected in the peaceful water.
The damp wood smells rich as I stand waiting
Inside the hollow insides of the horse.
Trojans are heaving on the rough, coarse rope
Hauling it into the city.
Laocoon's spear is vibrating by my left side,
But I daren't move.
The warm breath is closing up against my cheek
As though my whole body is steaming up.
Tears have formed in my eyes because the
Pain in my chest is unbearable.
My heart is pounding inside my body
Against my chest, like a hammer.
Blood is dripping into pools where dead bodies lie.
Trojans are screaming painfully as they die very suddenly.
The acrid smell of smoke, drifting in the air
As I walk down to the welcoming ship.
Ships at Greece are coming to greet us,
To hear about our victory
And celebrate with the men of our country.

Emily Hollingsworth (11)
Chaddlewood Junior School

DANCING FLOWERS

Flowers dancing to and fro,
Through the heavy, drifting snow.
What do they do in spring?
Well, what they do is dance and sing.

Flowers swiftly floating by,
Dancing, singing, in the sky.
Soaring higher than a bird,
Singing the song, Beethoven's Third.

Roses budding here and there,
Dancing with their lady fair.
Daffodils walking by,
Saying, 'hello' and 'hi'.

Natalie Brown (9)
Chaddlewood Junior School

THE SIEGE OF TROY

The strain in the carpenter's face as
He hauls the huge, splintering planks of wood around.
The musty air inside our ingenious idea, the Trojan Horse,
The fear in the other soldiers' black, misty eyes.
The hisses and splashes as the serpents rise out of the deep blue sea
And wrap their slimy, wet bodies around Laocoon and his two sons.
The bad odour of the sweaty Trojans in the air
As they haul the huge wooden horse into the city of Troy,
The wooden horse slowly lurching on squeaky wheels
Along the bumpy dirt track.
The heave-ho, heave-ho, as the Trojans struggle to
Haul the huge, splintering horse into Troy.
The sweat trickling down my worried face and into my mouth
As I wait for every last person to fall asleep.
The taste of blood as I thrust my sword into a body
And it sprays everywhere.
The crackle as the city of Troy is blazing,
Red in flames, and disintegrating.
The acrid smell of smoke from the smouldering city of Troy.
Sweet victory as the last hut of Troy is razed to the ground.
The salty sea air as we sail home in our boat
And the cool breeze blows in my face.

Luke McCoy (11)
Chaddlewood Junior School

THE SIEGE OF TROY

The sea crashing against the rocks,
The fresh sea air on the breeze,
The burning of wood as the camp is razed to the ground,
The heat of fire on my skin.
Men shouting as they slowly row away from Troy.
A huge, wooden horse standing proudly,
The hissing of angry serpents as they rise from the sea,
The creaking of the old wooden gates opening,
The lovely smell of meats cooking on open fires.
The Trojans celebrating and praising the wooden horse.
Orange flames arising from Troy,
The Greek army celebrating their victory.

Gemma Kent (11)
Chaddlewood Junior School

WOLF - THE WIND

In the darkest of night,
Wolf, the wind, howls between the flats,
Snuffling in the deep shifts of snow,
Darting in the shadows, in-between the lights,
Pausing only to sniff in a bin and steal a piece of meat,
Shaking it as he sneaks away.
He rules the city,
But when the sun starts to rise,
Wolf disappears into his den.
Gone, till sunset that night.

Amanda Adler (10)
Chaddlewood Junior School

My Little Sister

My little sister is terrible because:

She jumped on the table,
She tormented the cat,
She gargled with some jelly
And spat in Mum's hat.

She skived off school,
She ran down the road,
She went to the pet shop
And bought a toad.

She went on the field
And dug a big ditch.
I like my little sister,
She is truly a *witch!*

Laura Kearley (10)
Chaddlewood Junior School

Waiting For Christmas

Children play in the snow,
People dancing all night long,
Children dancing with their friends,
Shining stars all around,
Pretty lights in the ground.
Skating in the snow,
Glowing cheeks all around,
People dancing all about,
Santa will soon be here.
Must go home for Santa to come,
With all the presents and all the fun.

Holly Marsh (9)
Chaddlewood Junior School

FOOTBALL CRAZY

Football is great,
It is really fantastic,
Every time I think of it,
I spring up like elastic.

I play in a team
Where we are all very keen
To become the best,
It's our dream.

Ben is our goalie,
He's as big as a bear,
When the opposition see him,
They're in for a scare.

We've got the best defence,
No team can get through,
Helped by a fast midfield,
Who tackle strongly too.

We get the ball and keep it,
Passing it to each other.
It goes up to the striker
And he scores yet another.

We've won most of our games,
We're doing really well.
With our success in recent weeks,
We can't wait for the bell.

There is no team that we now fear,
We'll beat them all with style.
At last all trophies will come here
And stay here for a while.

Daniel Taylor (10)
Chaddlewood Junior School

THE FOX COMES OUT AT MIDNIGHT

The fox comes out at midnight,
He comes to hunt, is prey,
The colours of his furry coat
Are ginger, white and grey.

The fox comes out at midnight,
He goes to look for tea.
He needs to find a big meal
To feed his whole family.

The fox comes out at midnight,
Creeping down the rabbit holes.
Slowly, quietly and carefully,
The hungry fox goes.

The fox comes out at midnight.
After he had caught his prey,
Scuffling back through the leaves,
Trying to find where his family should stay.

The fox comes out at midnight,
He starts to serve a meal,
They start to tuck into supper,
Never a finer feast, they feel.

The fox comes out at midnight,
The family start to doze.
Next morning they will be fresh,
For the night that comes and goes.

Rachel Harrison (11)
Chaddlewood Junior School

CAN I 'AVE ME

Can I 'ave me ball back?
Can I 'ave me ball?
Mister, Mister,
Chuck it over the wall!

Bouncing off the wall,
Bouncing on the floor
Bouncing off the roof,
Bouncing on the door.

Can I 'ave me ball back,
Can I 'ave me ball?
Missis, Missis,
Chuck it over the wall.

Staring at the ceiling,
Staring at the wall,
Oh keep me in for hours,
But,
Please, give me back me ball!

Courtney Richards (9)
Chaddlewood Junior School

GALLOPING STRANGER

Gallop, gallop, over the deserts, across the sandy plains.
Gallop, gallop, stroking your horse's sandy mane.
Stranger, stranger, what do you want? Who are you?
Stranger, stranger, are you my friend? Do you want to live with
me too?
Galloping stranger, you are welcome here.
Galloping stranger, thank you for whispering that secret in my ear.

Nicola Hodgson (9)
Chaddlewood Junior School

FRUITS

F resh, spiky pineapples, shaking in the wind,
R uby-red raspberries, tumbling out of a tub,
U pheld hands, reaching for the glossiest apples,
I ndigo blueberries being pushed into a pie,
T en tall palms with hairy coconuts falling to the ground,
S treaky ships sailing to collect the juiciest fruits of all time.

Alan Dickins (9)
Chaddlewood Junior School

CATS

Cats, cats, everywhere, on the table, on the chair.
Some various cats are extremely rare,
When they see dogs, their hair stands on end,
They all have spirited stares.
Cats like to climb the highest trees,
Lots of cats have fleas.
My cats have a passion for cheese.
Cats come in various colours,
Ginger, white and black cats,
Curled up inside a sack,
Chasing birds and rats,
Even fighting the alley cats.
They always find the warmest place,
Elegant and full of grace,
They always have a smile on their face.
They're owned by many people of various race.
My cat comes from outer space,
From a very hot and sunny place.

Leah Hodges (9)
Eggbuckland Vale Primary School

CLOUDS

Some white, some purple,
They make your heart pop.
They open the sky and let supply
The orange with red, tuck you in at night,
But with your light still on.
As they drift away
The clouds whisper out of sight,
They come around again to sight,
But with a slight gloom
And black covers the sky.
A better light comes out of nowhere.
The moon is out for the night
And a smile occurs on his face.

Ross Holmes (9)
Eggbuckland Vale Primary School

DOGS

Dogs, dogs, they are great,
Dogs, dogs are the best,
Dogs make people happy,
Dogs are cuddly too.
They make people laugh and play
To see the dog is there.
Dogs are cuddly,
They sometimes make people cry,
But I don't care what they do,
Because they are the best animals in the world
And they're my favourite animals.

Abbie Davey (9)
Eggbuckland Vale Primary School

THE TRAIN POEM

Trains can be pains,
They drive you insane,
You should have a claim
If your train is to blame.

If you are late
For a special date
Because the train's not on time,
As it came at half-past nine.

I wish the trains wouldn't delay
And come on time every day.
I love trains, but they can make you mad,
But all in all, they are not bad!

Robert Jane (10)
Eggbuckland Vale Primary School

MY AUNTIE CLAIRE'S PUB

There's a little pub in Stoke called the 'Indian Inn'
A warm welcome awaits to all who enter in.
The big smile from Claire is always the same,
Whether you're a local or a stranger without a name.
The food is great and so is the beer,
We always leave the pub in good cheer.

Then there's Murphy, he's everyone's mate,
But don't shout *taxi*, he will get in a state.
Lord and Master of all is domain,
With one big *woof*, he says come again!

Abby McBeath (9)
Eggbuckland Vale Primary School

FOOTBALL CRAZY, FOOTBALL MAD

Football, football is a beautiful game,
From kick-off to corners,
The aim is the same.
Score lots of goals as fast as you can,
To be champions all over this footballing land.

Michael Owen scores yet again
To set us off for a World Cup win.
Come on England, come on lads,
We can win it given half a chance.

With Beckham, Heskey, Scholes and goals,
The World Cup is ours and everyone knows.
The competition is tough
And it's going to be rough,
So bang in some goals
And we'll all be chuffed.

So come on England, come on lads,
Let's take on the rest, 'cause we are the best!
Formation and strategy, passes and goals,
Free kicks and headers will make all the goals.

Let's go to Korea, three lions and all,
With confidence and attitude
To triumph over all.
Stand up David Beckham, Scholesy and all,
For England is calling,
So heed her call!

Francis Shepherd (10)
Eggbuckland Vale Primary School

MY BEST FRIEND, JAKE

Pirates are mean,
Pirates are scary.

Some are as small as a bean
And some are very hairy,

But if you see a pirate
In the open sea

Close your eyes and think,
He's really just like me.

Not all of our pirate friends are cruel

They just need a home that
They are able to rule.

So why not invite him into your home
And offer him some tea and a scone?

The last time I saw one,
I did just that,

He smiled, shook my hand
And tipped his hat.

For he is now my best friend, Jake
And we are so very happy.

So why not join me in my quest?
It's up to you to do the rest.

Chris Brown (10)
Eggbuckland Vale Primary School

THE PECULIAR WEATHER

Colours here, colours there,
Shooting flowers everywhere,
The wonderful spring has finally arrived
And the whole world has come alive.

Then comes summer with all its fun,
On the sandy beaches under the sun.
Getting sand between my toes,
Putting suncream on my nose.

Crispy leaves everywhere
And all the trees become so bare.
Autumn sees birds fly away,
They won't be back until next May.

Winter brings the shade of white.
Huge, warm fires glowing bright.
Wrapping up warm to go outside,
The miserable grey clouds really wide.

Each season is good and bad,
Although they can make you really mad!

Reah Partridge (9)
Eggbuckland Vale Primary School

WHAT MAKES ME HAPPY . . .

Happy is what I like to be,
It's like sitting under my willow tree.
In summer the sun is so much fun,
When my friends and I play out in the sun.

We sit under the willow tree
Out of the sun,
With my friends, I have lots of fun.

We sit under the tree until it gets dark,
When they go to bed
I sit up and think of tomorrow,
And having a lark.

Jessica Daly (9)
Eggbuckland Vale Primary School

THE HARE AND THE RABBIT

The hare and the rabbit are best friends,
But who is the best?

They can run as fast as the wind.
The rabbit can jump right up into the clouds,
But who is the best?

The hare can hear danger from far away,
The rabbit can dig many deep burrows,
But who is the best?

The hare can fight,
The rabbit can bite,
But who is the best?

The hare can kick,
The rabbit can scratch,
But who is the best?

The hare is the best,
The rabbit is the best,
They are both the best
Because they are best friends.
Do you think so too?

Jodie Walker (10)
Eggbuckland Vale Primary School

TEACHER, TEACHER

Teacher, teacher was late today,
Due to his payment on his plate.

Teacher, teacher, come here quick,
I can't control my temper.

Teacher, teacher is not in today,
So we can have a day off hip hip hooray!

Teacher, teacher, I wasn't in yesterday
Due to my headache.

Teacher, teacher is not in today
Because he left this school yesterday.

Teacher, teacher don't sit down
You have got some bubblegum on your bum.

Teacher, teacher come here quick,
My desk has just been broken.

Teacher, teacher could I pop out?

Teacher, teacher I'm fed up,
I can't control my hiccups.

Teacher, teacher please come back,
I'm really going to miss you.

Toni-Marie Shepherd-Lewis (10)
Eggbuckland Vale Primary School

THE TREE

The green tree sways in the wind
With the leaves shining in the sun,
The nests of birds with eggs hatching,
New life in the big, wide world.

The trees beside it growing steadily,
Birds shelter their youngsters from the rain,
Baby birds trying to fly,
Younger birds learning to glide.

Matthew Trotter (9)
Eggbuckland Vale Primary School

Ten School-Children

Ten school-children standing in a line,
One got punched, then there were nine.

Nine school-children sitting on a gate,
One got pushed, then there were eight.

Eight school-children praying to Heaven,
One felt sick, that it left seven.

Seven school-children playing with sticks,
One broke his arm and then there were six.

Six school-children found a beehive,
One got stung, then there were five.

Five school-children playing with a door,
One jammed his finger, then there were four.

Four school-children climbing a tree,
One fell down, then there were three.

Three school-children sitting on the loo,
One got stuck, then there were two.

Two school-children, one is me and the other is you.
What can we do?

Dean Lavis (10)
Eggbuckland Vale Primary School

MY TEACHER

My teacher is Mrs Fortune,
She helps me an awful lot
And when I have a puzzled face,
I always say, 'What?'

She always tidies her desk,
But it gets messy after that.
She tells people to wipe their feet
On the big, black mat.

Her cupboard is a complete mess,
But she tidies it up
And when she's urging for some water,
She always puts it in a cup.

Becky Mannell (10)
Eggbuckland Vale Primary School

OUR PET DOG JAKE

My pet dog is called Jake,
He's as skinny as a rake.
We all love him to bits,
Even though he has us in fits.
He likes to have treats,
Because it's something to eat.
He does the Irish jig
And eats like a pig.
He likes to play ball
And drives us up the wall,
And when he is asleep,
We think he is so sweet.

Ryan Banks (9)
Eggbuckland Vale Primary School

SEASONS

The autumn leaves are falling
Upon the ground so bare,
They really look appalling,
But we don't really care.

Winter will be coming,
The trees will fall asleep,
Ready for springtime,
When the buds begin to peep.

Then we have the summer sun,
When it finally has begun.
Flowers in full bloom,
But it will all be over soon.

Ben Hunter (10)
Eggbuckland Vale Primary School

THE DRAGON

The dragon swings his mighty tail
And breathes gigantic flames.
The dragon's skin has smooth scales,
Glittering and shimmering.
The dragon is the size of a giant, his teeth
The size of a man and as sharp as a sword.
His wings are like tornadoes speeding through the air.
When the dragon glides through the sky,
The sound he makes is deafening.
The dragon strikes fear into a knight's heart,
But never has anyone caught the dragon,
Until the present day.

Robbie Noble (10)
Eggbuckland Vale Primary School

OWLS

I like owls because they are awake at night.
I like owls because they give rats a fright.
I like owls because they sleep during the day.
I like owls best when they come out to play.
I like owls and that's how it will stay.
I will like owls forever, I would say.

Nicholas Symons (10)
Eggbuckland Vale Primary School

GOODBYE NAN

I was only young
When you left this world.
I had good times with you
And wish you could have stayed by my side.
Mum said you would watch over me.
I will always love you, Nan,
Goodbye, I'll always remember you.

Samantha Wilkes (9)
Eggbuckland Vale Primary School

STEAM

The track was deserted, there was no one in sight,
Then along came an engine, as black as the night.

The pistons were pumping, the furnace was red,
As roaring along the sleepers it sped.

The boiler was burning, the pressure was high,
A cloud of steam blasted high to the sky.

Then I awoke from my brilliant dream
And wished all the trains were run by steam.

Alex Lee (10)
Eggbuckland Vale Primary School

SPEED

Speed can be quick,
Speed can be slow,
Sometimes speed is neither.
What I think is fast is Concorde.
What do you think is fast?
Is it a car,
Or
An aeroplane?
But whatever it is, it's fast!

Jason Lam (9)
Eggbuckland Vale Primary School

FIREWORKS

Fireworks are like flower buds,
Waiting to unfold,

And as the Catherine wheel begins to flame,
It's like whirling marigolds.

As screamers spread along the glittery sea of stars,
You feel like you are on a journey through space to Mars!

Emily Bowden (10)
Eggbuckland Vale Primary School

I Had A Cat

I had a cat, its name was Chunkey,
I painted it green and it looked funky.
And all it did was sit by the fire,
Which made his coat go stiff as a wire.
Now that poor cat, with his coat all funky,
Went out for a walk one summer's day,
Met a new friend and ran away.

Lisa Congdon (9)
Eggbuckland Vale Primary School

My Sister

My sister Bethany Rose
Has ten fingers, has ten toes.
She has small ears,
She has a small nose,
That's my sister, Bethany Rose.

Kirstin Dunn (9)
Eggbuckland Vale Primary School

My Nan

My nan smells like fresh bread,
My nan is like a gentle dolphin,
My nan looks like the most beautiful princess in the world,
My nan is as soft as silk,
My nan is as calm as the sea of tranquillity,
My nan is as loving as a puppy,
My nan sometimes forgets things,
I love my nan!

Catherine Casey (10)
Eggbuckland Vale Primary School

FOOTBALL

Football is a sport,
Like cricket and basketball.
I like to support
Plymouth Argyle.

My favourite players are:
Micky Evans, David Friio and Martin Phillips,
They all have a shiny new car,
They all are fabulous.

They all have a fat wallet
Because they are football players.
Micky Evans likes Wallace and Gromit,
So does Kevin Wills.

Jamie-Lee Crockett (10)
Eggbuckland Vale Primary School

THE SUN

The sun is hotter than McDonald's hottest bun,
And a just-fired gun,
It's so hot, it's no fun!
My mum likes it because it helps her tan
And it heats my hot cross bun
And gives me a good beat from the heat
And it dries my sheets.
It dries out the meat for my bread.
After that busy day, I go to bed to rest my head.

Jake Cooper (10)
Eggbuckland Vale Primary School

MY HOUSE

My house is wide,
The furniture is cosy
And there I laid
In bed so dozy.

My house is big,
There is always light,
There wouldn't be a twig
Anywhere in sight.

I like my home,
It's perfectly fine.
The walls aren't made of foam
And this house is mine!

Charlotte Jackson (9)
Eggbuckland Vale Primary School

ANIMALS IN THE JUNGLE

Animals in the jungle,
What do they do?
Snakes slither and slide,
Tigers leap and jump,
Lions roar and eat,
Like animals do.
Monkeys swing from tree to tree,
Elephants wave their ears and
Spiders eat insects.

Cody Marley (10)
Eggbuckland Vale Primary School

UP IN THE BOUGHS OF THE GREAT OAK TREE

Trees whisper as I pass,
Waving their branches gently around.
I look up and see the golden leaves
Up in the boughs of the great oak tree.

As I walk under the great oak tree,
I hear a rustling sound.
A squirrel jumps from branch to branch,
Up in the boughs of the great oak tree.

I've seen the squirrels in the great oak tree,
But now I hear a tweeting sound,
And as I turn around, I see a tiny robin,
Up in the boughs of the great oak tree.

I've had such a brilliant time,
Now I must go home,
But I'll never forget the day I spent
Under the boughs of the great oak tree.

Beth Dymond (10)
Eggbuckland Vale Primary School

MY BUDDY

He jumps on me, he slobbers on me,
He's got a coat that's covered in fleas.
He growls at me when he's not jolly,
He's tiny compared to next door's collie.
Once he bit me on the nose,
Once he jumped on our prize-winning rose.
He gets my bum all wet and muddy,
But really, my dog's my best buddy.

Joe Shill (10)
Eggbuckland Vale Primary School

THE CLOCK

At the bottom of the stairs stands a very old clock,
Tick-tock, tick-tock, says the clock.

The hands slowly move around its shining face.
Even though it is old, it stands proudly waiting to be seen.

Its coating is shiny and looks polished.

It is getting ready to strike for midnight.
At last it has struck.

All over again, it stands very proud.
Tick-tock, tick-tock, says the clock.

Jasmine Lawry-Lovidge (9)
Eggbuckland Vale Primary School

PUFFIN

I know a pony,
Puffin is her name,
I know that it's a funny name,
But I like her all the same.

Her grey coat is shiny,
Her eyes are big and round,
I like to ride her
In country or in town.

Laura Edyveane (9)
Eggbuckland Vale Primary School

MY MUM

My mum is lovely,
My mum is kind,
She is my mum
And she's all mine.

She's thoughtful and caring,
Always there for me,
Convincing and sharing,
She will always be.

A mum in a million,
She's soft to the touch.
A mum in a million,
I love her so much.

Christopher Stribley (10)
Eggbuckland Vale Primary School

GREEN

Green is the grass,
Green is a tree,
Green is an apple,
Green is a grape,
Green is a cactus,
Green is the stem on a plant,
Green is a football shirt,
Green is a frog,
Green is a snake.

Jack Broadhurst (9)
Eggbuckland Vale Primary School

Dogs!

All dogs are big and small,
Can I have a dog that's tall?
I want a dog that's thin
And one which doesn't make a din.

I don't want a dog that's scary
And definitely not hairy!
I hope my dog is white
And keeps me warm at night.

I can't wait for its first walk,
I want my dog to talk.
I hope it doesn't always sleep
And I don't want it to chase sheep.

I know my dog is going to know
How its life should go
And now it's time for me to go!

Nicholas Sinnett (9)
Eggbuckland Vale Primary School

My Dad

M is for missing,
Y is for yearning,

D is for Dad,
A is for absence,
D is for distance, when my dad is at sea.

Reanne Letts (9)
Eggbuckland Vale Primary School

WHO, WHAT, WHERE, WHY, HOW?

What is school?
The education factory.

What is the universe?
The planet's yard.

What is a clock?
The face of time.

What are stars?
The holes in the sky.

What is birth?
The beginning of death.

Matthew King, Michael Martin & Geordie White (11)
High Street Primary School

MY MUM

She is a comfy cushion,
She is a black and white, cuddly panda,
She is the seaside,
She is the beach,
She is the song of a chirping bird on a spring morning,
She is Christmas, a jolly Christmas, full of joy,
She is a queen.

Josie Dunne (9)
High Street Primary School

MY GRANDAD

He's a bouncy bed,
He's a young, fierce lion,
He's Toys 'R' Us,
He's a barking dog at night,
He's afternoon of the day,
He's a best-seller.

Christopher Pinn (9)
High Street Primary School

THE CRESCENT MOON

The crescent moon is like
A glittery, silver bowl.
Look up high in the sky
And you will see
A bright, silver moon.
The changing moon is like
A kindly smile beaming down to Earth.
Look up high in the sky
And you will see
A bright, silver moon.
The waxing moon is like
A silver banana floating down.
Look up high in the sky
And you will see
A bright, silver moon.
The dying moon is like
It has no light, except night.
Look up high in the sky
And you will see
A bright, silver moon.

Syeda Kobir (8)
Hyde Park Junior School

THE NIGHT VIEW

A pearly expressionless face
Gazing down at the blue planet,
Rotating continuously.
Watch the night sky,
Watch the moon fly
Past the Earth and through
The night's kingdom.
An imposing button
Sewn into a black
Leather jacket like a dark
Blackboard of midnight.
A slice of an eyebrow
That is levitated up
Into a question mark.

Oliver Burton (9)
Hyde Park Junior School

THE MOON

The changing moon is like a silver banana
Floating in the night sky.
The waxing moon is like a silver bow of light,
Breaking through a black blanket.
The crescent moon is like a silver smile
Flying in the pitch-black sky.
The waning moon is like a banana
Hanging in the midnight sky.
The dying moon is like a sieve,
Sieving out the stars.

Adam Oats (9)
Hyde Park Junior School

THE MOON

The full moon is like a white face gazing on the world
Like a glossy bubble hanging in the night sky,
Like a misty crystal ball telling your future.

Watch the night sky,
Watch the moon fly,
Past the Earth and
Through the night's kingdom.

Like a shadowed firework towering over you,
Like a sandy biscuit,
Like a foggy eyeball covered in ice,
Like a glittering pearl shining in total darkness.

Watch the night sky,
Watch the moon fly,
Past the Earth and
Through the night's kingdom.

Bethany Rogers (9)
Hyde Park Junior School

THE FULL MOON

The full moon is an ice-covered Earth,
Reflecting the blazing flames owned by the sun.
Like an empty globe waiting for life,
Like a foggy eyeball, ready to fill the body,
Like a shiny crystal Earth
Glistening like it wants to be a star,
Like a pearl wanting to get in its clam,
Like a silver coin returning to the stars,
Thinking they're coins.

Josh Bunch (9)
Hyde Park Junior School

THE MOON

The full moon is
Like a white face gazing at the world,
A speckled marble rolling on a black carpet,
Like a sparkly top of lipgloss on a black, shiny cloth,
Like a reflecting crystal ball telling the future,
Like a biscuit in an African child's hand,
Like an empty globe hovering in the sky,
Like a misty Christmas bauble in a midnight-black handbag.

The changing moon is like
A happy smile on an African child's face.
The waxing moon is like
A gleaming phone hanging on an ebony hook.
The crescent moon is like
A Cheshire cat beaming at you.
The waning moon is like
A silver 'C' on a piece of black card.
The dying moon is like
A banana split being eaten by the child.

Connie Watson (9)
Hyde Park Junior School

THE MOON

The full moon is
Like a white face gazing on the world,
Like a colossal ball of cheese,
Like an ice elephant, grey, shining on the Earth,
Like a crystal disco ball,
Like a speckled, empty globe,
Like a pearl reflected by the sun,
Like a sandy-coloured bauble alone on a tree.

Lauren Clark (9)
Hyde Park Junior School

A RIDDLE

What am I?
I am a bit of broken, glowing glass.
I am a glowing banana, floating in space.
I am a gleaming telephone hanging on an ebony hook,
What am I?
(The crescent moon.)

Ella Kenny (8)
Hyde Park Junior School

WHAT AM I?

I am a silver needle being threaded into the sky.
I am a knife cutting the air.
I am a baby's crib rocking in the night.
What am I?
(The crescent moon.)

Lauren Phillips (8)
Hyde Park Junior School

THE MOON

What am I?
I am a glowing banana, eaten by the night.
I am a silver fighting blade, with a black handle.
I am like a kind smile, beaming down on Earth.
What am I?
(The crescent moon.)

Michael Warran (8)
Hyde Park Junior School

CAN I WRITE A MOON POEM?

The full moon is
Like a white-painted face,
Like a set of fireworks in the sky,
Like a sandy, ginger biscuit,
Like an ice-covered Earth,
Like a floating air bubble in the sky,
Like a silver coin in a velvet black purse,
Like a golden plate waiting to be used on a black tablecloth.

Moon, moon,
Shining moon,
Shine so bright
Like a little light.

Francesca Green (9)
Hyde Park Junior School

THE MOON

The full moon is
Like a white faze gazing on the world,
Like a speckled sphere hanging on the dark night,
Like a colossal bauble floating on the misty dark night,
Like a foggy eyeball glittering in the night sky,
Like a glossy silver coin dropping in the midnight purse.

Shining moon, glowing moon,
Why do you gleam like a shiny spoon?

Oscar Mo (8)
Hyde Park Junior School

THE SILVER MOON

The white, silvery exploding face,
Peeping down at the Earth,
Going round slowly.
A silver face,
A large, big, 5p coin,
Put onto the big coat of night.
Silver face,
A bit of silver eyebrow
That is raised up into
A bubble looking down.
A wheel,
Riding high,
Edged in silver space.

Samuel Burgess (8)
Hyde Park Junior School

THE MOON

The changing moon is like
A silver banana floating in the night sky.
The waxing moon is like
A button being pulled out of a pocket.
The full moon is a hole
Cut out of the night sky.
The crescent moon is like
A Jaffa Cake being eaten.
The waning moon is like
It's on wire, but the wire gets cut.
The dying moon is like a stone
Sinking into the deep depths of the sea.

Thomas Stenhouse-Pyne (9)
Hyde Park Junior School

THE MOON

I am a crystal boomerang hanging in the sky,
I am a bent Roman sword,
I am a golf ball thrown into the sky by the Lord,
I am a farmer's tool,
I am a light bow shot into a black blanket,
I am a banana in the black night.
What am I?
(The moon.)

Connor Legg (8)
Hyde Park Junior School

TREASURE, TREASURE EVERYWHERE

Treasure,
Treasure,
Everywhere,
It could be here,
It could be there.
Hidden high
And hidden low,
You could find it wherever you may go.
You could find it by the sea,
You could find it by the lake,
It could be real, it could be fake.
Treasure,
Treasure,
Everywhere.
It could be here,
It could be there.

Ben Robins (10)
Langley Junior School

ISLAND OF PLEASURE

On an island far away from land
Lies a treasure chest under hot quicksand.
No one dares to steal the gold,
Only someone who's very bold.

This wasn't just an island of treasure,
It was also an island of pleasure,
With lovely palm trees
And lots of beautiful seas.

A sailor coming across the sea
Saw the island and brave was he.
He decided to risk this dangerous part of the land,
Then without noticing, he disappeared into the hot quicksand.

Bethany Jagger (8)
Langley Junior School

HIDDEN TREASURE

Woof, woof,
I cried with all my might.
Woof, woof,
I need my bone tonight!

Woof, woof,
Oh no, I've gone way too far.
Woof, woof,
Oh look, I found a toy car!

Woof, woof,
Yes, I've got my hidden treasure.
Woof, woof,
Oh yes, what a pleasure!

Layla Ahmadi (10)
Langley Junior School

TOOTH FAIRY

My tooth started to wiggle,
My tooth started to shake,
Suddenly my tooth came out,
Like a really fast earthquake!

That night I put it under my pillow,
Not long after that I went to sleep.
I was dreaming of lots of happy things
And I did not make a sound, not a peep.

A light came into my room,
Like a really bright sun,
Coming was the tooth fairy,
Being a tooth fairy must be lots of fun!

I woke up in the morning,
My tooth had disappeared,
I was stretching and yawning
And a very shiny treasure had appeared!

Carly Johnson (7)
Langley Junior School

THE TREASURE

Under the deep blue sea,
Something waits for me.
Under the deep blue sea,
What can it be?
Under the deep blue sea,
I see a sparkling tree.
What can it be?
The treasure waits for me.

Annie Ingram (8)
Langley Junior School

MY HIDDEN TREASURE

My sister is my treasure,
She brings me so much pleasure.
Her eyes are like jewels, they shine so bright,
When she's angry, they give me a fright!

My sister is my treasure,
We play a lot together.
We sit on our bunk beds at the top
And think what we'll be when we grow up.

My sister is my treasure,
I think she's rather clever.
She sits on my lap and reads aloud,
Oh how I'm so very, very proud.

My sister is my treasure,
Our love we cannot measure.
She is hidden deep within my heart,
I hope we will never be apart.

My sister is my treasure,
I will love her forever.
The best treasure you will ever find
Is a sister who's loving and kind.

Sarah Hill (10)
Langley Junior School

HIDDEN TREASURES

Hidden treasures
Under the sea,
Under the ground,
In the sand,
All around.

Hidden treasures
In your house,
In your room,
Under your bed,
All around!

Lauren Hall (10)
Langley Junior School

WHERE HAVE YOU HIDDEN IT?

Is it under the sea
Buried in deep sand,
Is it hidden in a sunken ship
That used to be grand?

Is it locked up in a tower
That is guarded by a dragon,
Is it hidden by a cowboy
Who drives a dusty wagon?

Is it hidden up a tree
Where nobody goes,
Is it sat on by an ugly troll
With stinky, mouldy toes?

Is it floating in the ocean
Or swallowed by a whale,
Is it sitting on a puffy cloud
Or in a huge, windy gale?

It is none of these places
It's buried by the tree,
In my mate's back garden
Is my dad's car keys!

Sophie Donovan (8)
Langley Junior School

MY MISSION

I'm on a mission
To find a necklace.
It belongs to my nan.
It's blue with a gold chain.

I start to go down,
It's getting darker,
I'm a bit nervous,
I switch my torch on.

Wow! I see
Big shapes, little shapes,
Catfish, angelfish,
Baby fish and big fish.

I dive a bit deeper,
I see something blue.
It looks exactly like the one on the necklace.
It has a chain, but I don't think it is gold.

I carry on swimming deeper.
I can't find the other divers,
They might have left me, or
Even worse, gone home and . . . and . . .

'Are you OK?' said one of the divers.
'Who were you talking to?' he said.
'Oh no, don't worry.
Come on, let's go.'

'I really want to find it.'
'You won't at this speed.'
'Are we going to carry on?'
'No, let's go home.'

Emily Laverick (10)
Langley Junior School

Now, That's A Treasure Hunt

In the middle of the window,
Shouting out for the fit and clever,
The massive poster stated,
Treasure hunt, the biggest ever.

They gathered under the sky
At the beginning of that fab day,
When the loudspeaker crackled,
'Come to the red clues desk straight away.'

All the clues given out,
They were waiting for the starter's sign,
Everything is silent,
Everyone runs to the long, white line.

The treasure hunt had started.
The first off were Samantha and Shabos,
Everyone had followed,
Now everyone had gone with clues.

Follow the large, pretty signs,
Look high in the sky, down to the ground,
A lolly stick and feather,
All of these must be found.

'Look at that hole,' said Ronald.
As his hand was sliding down the hole,
He felt something cold and smooth.
Ronald thought it was a piece of coal.

Ronald thought and thought and then
Sam passed the shovel to Ronald.
He dug and dug on that hole,
And then he saw it . . . solid gold!

Louise Elford (9)
Langley Junior School

HIDDEN TREASURE

Shooting down a tunnel,
Flame dripping from his jaws,
Looking for hidden treasure,
Lying underneath the floors.

Sniffing at the musty air,
Smelling the treasure resting near,
Getting closer, closer, closer,
Letting loose a toothy sneer.

Pounding the ground and clawing,
Greedy for the awaiting sight,
Only he knows what he'll find,
Is it worth all the plight?

Finally he breaks through the rock
And admiring his precious hoard,
He lies down for his rest,
Claws grasping at a sword.

Kathryn Langston (11)
Langley Junior School

I DREAM

I dream of having a dolphin
That swims in the sea
And a huge mansion,
As beautiful as can be.

I dream of having a horse
That I could ride
And be on holiday with my family,
Side by side.

I dream of having a theme park
That I could play on all day,
I dream of having all of these,
But will they come true?
They may!

Robyn Lunt (9)
Langley Junior School

HIDDEN TREASURES

If I had a treasure,
I'd be as rich as a queen!
With jewels all around me
And a smile like a beam.

A dog's would be a bone,
Worth nothing but a penny,
But the money to a dog
Would be worth many and many.

If a monkey would have a choice,
He'd choose for a fellow friend,
For them to scratch and play with each other
And there would never be an end.

But there's still one problem
Which is a little too big!
That's where to find the treasure
And that's not a fib
That's bad to tell.

Caroline Clark (10)
Langley Junior School

HIDDEN TREASURE

I am dozing and I'm dreaming
Of a treasure far away.
I'm thinking of a sandy beach
To visit again one day.

I am scurrying and I'm searching
Upon the golden grain,
I'm feeling for a roughened shell,
That will be dark and plain.

I am clutching and I'm clinging
To a shell I've found, it's mine.
I am opening the present,
That cushion's something fine.

I am revealing and receiving
A gift entirely free,
Found upon a sandy beach,
It was meant for only me.

It is sparkling and it's shining,
In its bed that is a shell.
Seen there for the first time,
With a fairy tale to tell.

I am wriggling and I'm waking,
The morning's just begun.
I was dreaming of a treasure,
Somewhere foreign in the sun.

Anna Rashleigh (10)
Langley Junior School

HIDDEN TREASURE

Underneath the shade of blue,
There's a big shadow of you.
On the sand, brown and bold
Is some treasure that's solid gold.
Someone sailing, it is you,
So stop pretending, your dream is not true.

Stephanie Pearce (10)
Langley Junior School

LUCY

When Lucy walks into the wardrobe,
She becomes a trembling coat-remover.
When she comes out of the wardrobe,
She becomes a wide-mouth face-astonisher.
When she is looking at something,
She becomes an open-mouthed examiner.
When she walks in the snow,
She becomes a trembling, crunching walker.
When she talks to the Queen,
She becomes a quivering chatterer.
When she comes out of the wardrobe the other side,
She becomes a Mr Tumnus-lover.
When the dwarf asks her questions,
She becomes a shivering-quiverer.
When she goes to the professor,
She becomes an excited hand-waving waver,
And when she is scared,
She becomes a frightened worrier.

Kerry Shilson (10)
Montpelier Junior School

COMPUTER GOES SHOPPING

Computer rolls
To the electronic door.
Its program hums
As it enters the superstore.
Its VDU screen
Flickers and blinks,
Pausing at each aisle,
It puzzles and thinks:
6 CD-ROMS
and circuit boards,
a brand new mouse,
that needs to be insured.
Colour printer,
Plus a scanner,
Could do with micro-chips,
Especially a planner.
Computer can't find anything,
Only cauliflower and cheese,
Let me find something,
Oh please, oh please!
Red, angry and fists curled,
Goes to the shop assistant,
'Where's PC World?'

Caroline George (11)
Montpelier Junior School

TOOTY FROOTY

For breakfast it's a melon,
For lunchtime it's a lemon,
For teatime it's a cherry,
For supper it's a berry.

I always reach for a peach
But end up with a pear.
Those raspberries make a lovely crumble,
But strawberries make my tummy rumble.

Louise Stewart (10)
Montpelier Junior School

BEFORE I . . .

If you don't get your coat on
Before the time I count to ten,
You won't have dessert after tea.
One . . .
But I can't find it.
Two . . .
It's by the back door.
Three . . .
It's not there.
Four . . .
Yes it is.
No it isn't.
Five . . .
I don't want to see Grandma.
Tough luck, six . . .
Is it in your room? Seven.
Eight . . .
Found it!
Nine . . .
Put it on.
Ten . . .
We're off!

Chelsey Lindup (10)
Montpelier Junior School

INSIDE MY HEAD

In it there is a vet
And animals,
For banning homework forever.

And there is
The Titanic,
Which shall come last.

And there is
A new beefburger,
A new big-screen TV,
A new type of dog.

There is a big ball of string,
About five feet tall.
There is an invisible chocolate machine
And only I know where it is.

There is a wand for disappearing parents,
There is a new programme of The Simpsons.

In it, there is a PlayStation
And an alien,
Which is burning all our schoolwork. Yeah!

And part of a movie
Which is really cool,
Killing people, blood everywhere.

And there is a cuddly bear and lots of Beanies which come alive,
And there is a secret admirer on Valentine's Day,
And there are a million eggs at Easter.

And there is an
Entirely new micro scooter,
An entirely new pair of rocket boots,
An entirely new stunt bike.

I believe everybody has an imagination
And every body dreams, but
Not every body thinks as hard as others.

Melissa Curtis (11)
Montpelier Junior School

THE SNARK

Be wary of the awful snark
That waits under your bed,
Until it is so very dark
That he can see your head.

His eyes are boiling, lava red,
And his hands - ogre green,
He'll make sure that his stomach's fed
By gobbling up your spleen.

He'll grab you by your curly hair
And lift you off the ground,
Transport you to his dingy lair,
Where you will not be found.

Keep a watch for this ugly beast,
Hiding in clouds of mist,
Or you might end up as his feast,
If you don't get my gist.

Mark Wilson (10)
Montpelier Junior School

MY BROTHER

He comes home from school,
He's a bag-thrower, a loud, moaning mumbler.
When he sits at the table
He's a food-player, a drink-gobbler.
A stair-stomper,
A hard homework-doer,
He's a loud music player,
A ceiling-shaker,
A rap singer,
A PlayStation player.
When he's with me
He's a big wrestler, a giant,
With a bundle of new submissions.

Edward Privett (10)
Montpelier Junior School

RECIPE FOR A DREAM

Take a paradise island
And a lot of sunshine,
Add in adventure, bits of magic,
Magnificent kings and evil queens.
Sprinkle with fun and enjoyment,
Magical creatures, fairies and tiny elves,
Cover with happy smiles
And wrap in layers of sleep and darkness
To remember in the morning.

Leanne Earnshaw (10)
Montpelier Junior School

MY BROTHER

He comes home as a big-mouth swearer,
A bag-throwing stupid brother.
When he gets to his room,
He's a TV-watcher, couch-flapper,
A food-eating, juice-drinking guzzler.
He's a can't-be-bothered-toy-breaker,
A cheeky-mouthed mumbler,
A screaming loud-mouth moaner,
Eating Chinese on Saturday.
He's a pizza-lover,
An excited football-watcher.
In the kitchen, he's a roast potato-muncher.
At home, he's my brother.
Really, he's a family-lover,
A daft, dumb brother with a grumpy face.

Nathan Biship (10)
Montpelier Junior School

RECIPE FOR A DREAM

Take an imaginary world
And a tall castle,
Add a heroic dwarf, gigantic trolls,
A hero and a skilful wizard.
Sprinkle with strong axes and sharp swords,
Bold kings, brave knights and beautiful fairies,
Cover with terrific battles
And wrap in the happy ending
To remember on the hurtful days.

Elliot Hugh (10)
Montpelier Junior School

CINDERELLA

Cinderella, Cinderella,
I guess that Prince Charming
Is a real, nice fella.
I hear he's a real cool guy,
He has a palace up in the sky.
He wears a suit
And best of all, he plays the flute,
Which brings him lots of money.
If you go to the ball, you could be his honey!
You will win his hand in marriage
And you will ride in a golden carriage.
He will sing a love song to you,
Just because you went too!

Philippa Starr (8)
Montpelier Junior School

RECIPE FOR A DREAM

Take a sleepy baby
And an adventure,
Add a spooky castle, bewitched queens,
Evil kings and everlasting doughnuts.
Sprinkle with pharaohs and princes,
Scary ogres, magical dream worlds and
Cute, fluffy animals.
Cover with creamy milkshake
And wrap in Heaven,
To remember next night.

Grant Kennedy (10)
Montpelier Junior School

THE SNARK

Be wary of the spooking snark
That lurks beneath the floor.
When it's time for bed and dark,
Don't look behind the door.

The snark's favourite time is night,
Where it lurks in the shadows deep.
It'll come behind and give you a fright,
While you're in your deep sleep.

He'll pull out your hair with a ping,
And click go your toes,
Swallow you up with its mouthy-thing,
Then does a burp and goes.

So watch your steps when next
You go at sunset to the park,
Or you might end up in the closet below
As supper for the snark.

Katie Wall (10)
Montpelier Junior School

WHAT IS A PUPIL?

A plate of jelly that can't keep still,
A chatterbox who laughs and talks all day,
A caterpillar munching through its work,
A tornado who destroys everything in one wet play time,
An acrobat who swings to a new idea,
A car, difficult to get started on an icy morning.

Nicola Gill (10)
Montpelier Junior School

DAD

Dad is the hairy monster,
Boisterous boxer, jolly joker.
The tennis player, toe-tickler,
Silly Billy, chin-prickler.
The dizzy-whizzy, spin-me-around,
Grizzly bear makes a roaring sound.
Football star, motor car,
Bucking donkey, cheeky monkey.

But sometimes he's
A 'Go-away-please,'
A snorty-sleeper, a snorey-slump,
An eyelid-dropper, a lazy lump.
I'm a puppet without a string,
Waiting for Dad to dance again.

Laura Browne (10)
Montpelier Junior School

RECIPE FOR A DREAM

Take a sleepy child
And a handsome prince,
Add a candy land, cake rain,
Riding unicorn and a gorgeous band.
Sprinkle with fairy dust and golden palaces,
Chewy sweets, hot chocolate and Teddy Land.
Cover with a plum sun
And wrap in a cosy duvet
To remember in the morning.

Jodie Davey (10)
Montpelier Junior School

EastEnders

The Queen Vic is a lovely place,
But Peggy Mitchell has a grumpy face.
Jamie is chucked out of Sonia's house,
She thinks he is a lazy louse.

Samantha's back from sunny Spain
And she is showing off again.
She takes Zoe into town
And buys her a sparkly gown.

Moe is scared of Trevor again,
She thinks he's going to cause her pain.
Harry has died, but no one cares,
Have you seen the earrings Pat wears?

Elisha Searl (9)
Montpelier Junior School

Recipe For A Dream

Take a sleepy child
And a warm, cosy bed,
Add a bit of comedy, spectacular magic,
A spooky castle,
Sprinkle with some surprises and action,
Pop stars, a dream land a couple
Of spooky dwarfs.
Cover with excitement and imagination
And wrap in a happy ending
To help you relax and forget your troubles.

Joseph Copp (10)
Montpelier Junior School

EastEnders

Walford is a fabulous place,
Peggy has a grumpy face,
Little Moe is scared of Trevor,
So she goes to court with her friend Heather.
Samantha gets all the boys,
So Janine goes home to play with her toys.
The Slaters are all in a fix,
They're all sat at home eating Twixs.
Jamie is kicked out of Sonia's house,
Then she kicks out a rotten old mouse.
Dot and Jim are getting wed . . .
Phew! I think I'll go to bed.

Abby Roberts (9)
Montpelier Junior School

Recipe For A Dream

Take a warm little boy
And a cosy duvet cover,
Add a few goblins,
Fluttering fairies, magic and rough castles.
Sprinkle with happy memories and
Imagination, delicate palaces,
Luck and a hero.
Cover with lots of adventure
And wrap in loving, tender care,
To keep the person safe and happy.

Sam Jailler (10)
Montpelier Junior School

SWEETS

It was then I dreamed
Of a huge pile of sweets,
Galaxy bars to crunch,
KitKats to break.

I sorted out the Mars bars,
Maltesers, Skittles,
Chocolate Buttons, millions,
All to cram into my mouth.

I filled my bag with
Liquorice, cherry drops,
Penny sweets and chocolate.

Out of the tin
I pulled some bubblegum,
Some raspberry gums
And some slithery chocolate snakes.

All in front of me was
Red, blue, green and yellow,
And every colour you could think of.

Autumn Widdison (11)
Montpelier Junior School

HAILSTORM

The hailstorm comes
Like an enraged bull.
It tramples cities and towns
On tree trunk legs
And then stammers on.

Natalie Dodd (10)
Montpelier Junior School

SHE WAS...

She was . . .
A girl,
A teenager,
A wife,
A mother.

She was . . .
Honest,
Never spiteful,
Good at bowling,
Good at badminton.

She was . . .
Forgetful,
Truthful,
Kind.

She was . . .
Never puzzled,
So strong,
Good worker,
Good mannered.

She was . . .
Extremely fast,
Had good qualities,
Had good respect.

She is . . .
My mum.

Demi Flack (10)
Montpelier Junior School

I REMEMBER

I remember the loud beat on the CD player,
A voice shouting, 'Go and get dressed, she'll be here in a minute!'
Walking somewhere, an unknown place,
A sharp feeling of excitement,
My heart beating.
Where am I going: I want to know.
This only happened a year ago.

I remember a scrape of a lock,
A yell of, 'She's here!'
I open my eyes, walk in,
Happy birthday blown in my face.
A blitz of balloons comes towards me.
Red, yellow, purple, orange.
Two presents on a table, you know,
This was only a year ago.

I remember two wrapped presents,
A birthday cake as I walked past.
I'm at the presents, looking at bright colours,
Red, green, black, silver.
First one open, a make-up set,
Second one open, a television.
I loved those presents for ages, you know,
This only happened a year ago.

That's all I can remember from a year ago,
The surprise birthday, you know.
A blitz of balloons,
Some birthday presents,
Being guided to it all,
This is as far as I remember, you know.
This birthday that happened a year ago.

Louise Rogers (10)
Montpelier Junior School

I REMEMBER

I remember the multicoloured presents
That beamed in my eyes when I woke up,
Only a year ago.

My tree twinkling in the darkness
Making the room light up as if
It was in the middle of a summer's day.
The mountain of presents that stood up
Behind the tree like a brick wall.
Not long ago.

I remember, you know, faces staring at me
And the smile of my Aunt Linda,
Pouring a glass of sparkling wine for herself,
And the cake that was so big it filled the table.
That's all I can remember from a year ago.

The tower of presents, the smile of my aunt,
The twinkling lights on my tree,
That special Christmas, just for me.

Gareth Mitchell (10)
Montpelier Junior School

MY CLASS

My class is one of the best,
With Corey and Curtis and all the rest.
I think my class is one of the best.
Aimee and Elisha are always doing dances,
They think they're good, but they're really 'prances.'
All the rest are cheering and waving,
That is why our class is the best at raving!

Ryan Upton (9)
Montpelier Junior School

PEOPLE

Evil people kill the innocent,
The wildlife suffers
While they wreak havoc.
Help me God not to be evil.

Rich people make the poor suffer,
Say cruel words to their followers.
Some rich people are nice,
Lord, let me be good.

Good people stretching God's love,
Trying to make peace,
While healing the sick.
Oh Lord, give me this gift.

Rachael Hutchings (9)
Montpelier Junior School

THE BIG ONE!

T   he Big One is my best friend,
H   er name is Georgina,
E   very night I sleep with her,

B   ecause she's my best friend,
I   even take her to my gran's,
G   ran doesn't mind, she loves her too.

O   nly one person thinks she's horrid,
N   atasha is her name,
E   verybody doesn't know she is a monkey!

Jessica Coles (8)
Montpelier Junior School

THE HOUR WHEN THE WITCHES FLY

When night just turns stone cold,
When thunder booms in the sky,
When dead bodies fester and mould,
That's the hour when the witches fly.

When vampire bats go to suck blood,
When blood veins come to my eye,
When you hear a really loud thud,
That's the hour when the witches fly.

When gruesome vampires evolve into bats,
When you hear a strangled cry,
When you hear grey, scurrying rats,
That's the hour when the witches fly.

When your nightmare gets stuck in your head,
When you wake up and start to cry,
When out jumps the ghost from under your bed,
That's the hour when the witches fly.

Emmalene Massey (9)
Montpelier Junior School

FOOTBALL CRAZY

F   ootball is so great,
O   h yes,
O   h yes, it is.
T   ry not to get a yellow card,
B   ut try and break their legs,
A   gainst the rules they say it is,
L   uis Figo gets the shots,
L   igo scores the goals!

Daniel Evans (9)
Montpelier Junior School

MONTPELIER PLAYGROUND BLUES

The wind is cold, the sky is grey,
But we're still told to go out and play.

My teacher's in class, I bet he's not cold,
Sitting near a radiator, I wish I was old.

I stand here alone, a chill in my toes,
My best friend's inside, she's got a cold nose.

There's homework tonight, so much to be done,
No time for resting, no time for fun.

The bully's at home, I think she's got flu,
I want to go home and be sick too.

We've a spelling test next and a score to beat,
I get told off because I cheat.

Colder than ever, I'm coughing and wheezing,
Can't wait to go in, because outside it's freezing.

Rosie O'Donnell (11)
Montpelier Junior School

RECIPE FOR A DREAM

Take a tired person
And a long, deep sleep,
Add great kings and queens and nice people,
Big adventures and lots of fun.
Sprinkle with great places and good times,
To meet famous people, to go to paradise
And fly high in the sky,
Cover with a great imagination
To remember your dream in the morning.

Jessica Burling (9)
Montpelier Junior School

EastEnders

The Vic is a lovely place
But Peggy has a grin on her face.
Jamie got thrown out of Sonia's house
And went round the back, as silent as a mouse.

Samantha is chatting up the boys
And goes into town to buy a toy.
Someone called Harry has died, but they don't care,
Samantha buys a pair of shiny slippers,
And buys Phil some sparkly flippers.
Sam is back on the road,
She has to carry a heavy load.

Nicola Richmond (9)
Montpelier Junior School

Recipe For A Dream

Take a world you can eat
And an exciting new adventure,
Add a laugh, layers of happy times,
Great mysteries and agent solving.
Sprinkle with merry elves and miniature dwarves,
Green goblins, fairy tale creatures
And the best ever friend.
Cover with a sparkle of stars
And wrap in a happy ending,
To remember in the morning.

Katie Saunders (9)
Montpelier Junior School

SOMETHING I REMEMBER

I'll tell you, shall I, something I remember?
Everybody was excited, my eagerness inside,
In a rush down the stairs,
Tripping, I curled into a ball at the bottom,
Then nothing.
Pains striking down my back,
My eyes melted into waterfalls,
Paralysed.

I remember Mum, rushing after me,
Dizzy, very dizzy.
I could feel blood draining from my body,
Slowly trying to pick myself up to my feet,
Pain running through my body.
I remember this Christmas,
Because it was the year I broke my toe.

Jack Wilson (11)
Montpelier Junior School

RECIPE FOR A DREAM

Take an adventure
And a magical land,
Add a unicorn, a beautiful princess,
Magical elves and a handsome prince.
Sprinkle with sunshine and chocolate rain,
Fluffy pink candyfloss, chocolate ships and candy doors.
Cover with happiness
And wrap in a cloud for my duvet,
To remember in the morning.

Samantha Wilkinson (9)
Montpelier Junior School

MY BROTHER

My brother is the football maniac,
The wrestling fan, the racing fanatic,
The moody guts, the tell-tale tit,
The loud voice, the annoying nit,
The fussy eater, the early bird,
Loves jam, hates lemon curd,
Is very strong, like King Kong.

But sometimes he's a
Snoring sleeper, lazing lump,
A resting wreck, a snoozing slump,
And I'm a pencil without a lead
Waiting for him to get out of bed.

Rebecca Myers (11)
Montpelier Junior School

RECIPE FOR A GOOD DREAM

Take a sleeping baby
And a comfortable bed,
Add a friend to play with
And a piece of sun.
Sprinkle with icing and
Chocolate rain.
Go back to ancient Egypt
With the pharaoh,
Cover with Smarties
And wrap in gingerbread men,
To remember when you wake up.

Thomas Morley (9)
Montpelier Junior School

THE BLARK

Be wary of the sneering blark
Who hides behind your door.
He lies in wait where it is dark,
Or hides beneath your floor.

His thoughts are black as darkest night,
His teeth are bogey green.
He likes to give small children a fright,
Beware! He's really mean!

He'll grab your head and rip it off,
Your bones he'll grind and crunch,
He really thinks that he's a boff,
Gobble, gobble, munch!

So watch out when you next go to
Your bedroom for a sleep.
The blark'll be waiting for you,
To make you cry and weep!

David Hazeel (11)
Montpelier Junior School

THE HIDDEN GREAT WHITE SHARK

The hidden Great White shark,
Down deep in the sea,
No one has seen it but me.
It never comes up to the shore,
It only eats people for dinner,
Then it goes down below in the deep, dark ocean,
And never looks any thinner.

Curtis Mason (8)
Montpelier Junior School

THE BATTLE OF THE JADE DRAGON

The dragon is dead,
No longer will it fly,
Or raise its proud head
To look towards the sky.
It was doing no harm,
Just resting from the long flight,
But along came a dragon-slayer to disturb his calm.
The Jade Dragon was old and he could not fight.

The land is dead,
Black clouds cover the sky,
Sorrow is in everyone's head,
The dragon-slayer has everything he can buy.
Much harm did the king do,
And instead of getting fame,
He should suffer for his selfishness
And should hang his head in shame.

Anastasia Long (10)
Montpelier Junior School

BROTHERS

B   ossy and boasting,
R   otten and rude,
O   dd and over-excited,
T   icklish, squeamish,
H   orribly hitting,
E   vil, evil, evil,
R   otten and . . .
S   ickening.

Why did my mum have a baby *boy!*

Tilly Sampson (8)
Montpelier Junior School

I REMEMBER . . .

I'll tell you, shall I, something I remember?
Something that still means a great deal to me.
Not that long ago.

I remember asking my mum if I would ever leave here,
Smelling the mud from the river,
I still hear the river flowing.

I still feel the cow licking my boots clean,
Going down the muddy path,
Through the field in autumn.

I remember the big window at the front,
The patch of grass with a jungle at the back,
A giant's garden.

That is the best thing I remember,
It might mean nothing to you,
But it does to me.
Then I moved to here, you see.

Gemma Jones (11)
Montpelier Junior School

SISTERS

S   isters, sisters,
I   hate sisters.
S   isters are annoying,
T   hey hit you all day,
E   ven when you let them play.
R   otten sisters always tell,
S   ister you are horrible because you always smell!

Rhys Harrison (8)
Montpelier Junior School

CHANGING ROOM RAP

Walk into the changing room,
About to get dressed,
Step over the bags
And all the other mess.

Take off my tie,
Hang it on the peg,
Undo my shoes,
And take 'em off my leg.

Teachers stare around
And give a groan,
Cos this is the way
The teachers moan.

Hurry up, hurry up children,
The chatting has to stop.
You have a minute,
So get on your top.

Ok! Ok! I'm coming.
I don't want to miss the slide,
I've got on my top,
I'm coming for a ride.

Abi Hunns (11)
Montpelier Junior School

I THINK

Mum and Dad,
I think I've had
A bit too much to eat.
I also think Mum and Dad,
You have smelly feet.

Mum and Dad,
I think
The baby needs a bath.
I also think, Mum and Dad,
Friends should have a laugh!

Lucie Walker (11)
Montpelier Junior School

THE AWKERS

Watch out for the terrible Awkers,
They'll crawl under your door,
They'll eat you up like a bag of Walkers,
They get you when you're dead bored.

Their brains are packed with wit,
They eat you like cherry flan,
Then gobble you up, bit by bit,
And have always got a cunning plan.

They'll grab your hair and bite your legs
And snap you like a twig,
Then chew on you and swallow you like scrambled egg,
Munch, munch, gulp!

So when you are all alone in town,
You're on a beautiful walk,
You might end up falling in the pit down,
As victims for the terrible Awkers.

Nicholas Friend (11)
Montpelier Junior School

TOMMY

When Tommy set the school alight,
He giggled with great delight.
'Look how school's burning, Mum,
It makes the grass so bright!'

When Tommy played at 'tig',
Other children ran in fright,
For the hands Tommy had,
Were covered in dynamite.

When Mum took Tommy to the fair,
She prayed for sensible fun,
Her ideas changed when Tommy shot
A ride with his gun.

When Tommy found a giant rat,
He hit it on the head,
Then took it home to hide it,
Inside his mother's bed!

Sophie Roe (11)
Montpelier Junior School

FEET

Skating and shaking,
Running and dancing,
Tickling and itching,
Skidding on ice,
Feet.

Bethany Smith (7)
Montpelier Junior School

THE CLARK

Be careful of the killing Clark
That uses toys for bait.
It's waiting in the gruesome dark
And cruelly chooses fate!

Its spit is brown and freezing cold,
Its voice is very loud.
Its teeth are green and spread with mould,
Its breath is badly fouled.

He'll crack your bones for his toast
And cooks your skin for pastry,
He'll use your liver in his roast
And finds your eyes quite tasty.

So don't go down to the riverside
Without your mum and dad,
Otherwise your eyes might just get fried,
Which makes the Clark quite glad.

Joshua Blackwell (11)
Montpelier Junior School

JESSICA

J   essica is a lovely friend,
E   njoyable to me,
S   he tries not to argue,
S   he cares a lot for me.
I   f she has an accident, I'm there for her,
C   os she's there for me.
A   dorable Jessica, my very best friend.

Lauren Baker (8)
Montpelier Junior School

SHE WAS . . .

She was . . .
A baby,
A child,
A teenager,
A sister.

She was . . .
A good friend,
A rotten bowler,
Not bad at hockey.

She was . . .
Always in the mood for a hug,
Helping me with hard things,
First line in choir,
When I was upset, she was there.

She was . . .
Forgetful,
Funny,
Playful.

She was . . .
Always honest,
Enjoying Christmas,
The best.

She was . . .
My sister.

Jessica Ellard (11)
Montpelier Junior School

INSIDE MY HEAD

In it is a TV
And a thought
Of getting rid of school.

And there is
An idea of being a super hero,
To be able to fly over houses.

And there is
A new type of cheeseburger,
A new type of car,
A new type of hamster.

There is a video that plays backwards,
There is a cream that makes you invisible,
There is a drink that makes you the best at everything.

In it is a screen that tells you
What ideas you need for the next lesson.

And there is a song that you just
Can't stop singing over and over again.

There is an idea of having a pet lion
And a pet tiger.

I believe that everyone's head is like a kaleidoscope,
But instead of pictures moving around,
Your thoughts are moving around.

Holly Golden (11)
Montpelier Junior School

It Was Then I Dreamed

It was then I dreamed of
Music,
CDs to listen to,
Tapes to records.

I hear the notes play,
Crotchets, quavers,
High and low.

I place the CD
In the player,
The buttons
On the side,
The disc spinning,
Like a food mixer.

Conductors waving their arms,
In a figure of eight,
Conducting the choir in front of them.

It was then I dreamed of music.

The reed on a saxophone
Vibrates on my lip.

The notes rise, one by one, on the paper,
As,
Bs,
Fs
And Es.

I hear the songs
That my mum used to sing.
Rock 'n' roll and hip-hop!

Flutes, saxophones, clarinets,
Recorders, drums.

It was then I dreamed of music.

Rachael Onslow (11)
Montpelier Junior School

MY MUM

Mum is the enormous eater,
Sarcastic superstar, jolly joker,
Happy housekeeper, scary singer,
Laughing lady, the tickle finger.
She cooks the best tuna bake,
Along with her Christmas cake.

But sometimes she's a
'I-want-a-nap-please,'
A yawny mouth, a tired lump,
A snoring mum, all in a slump,
And I'm a fork without a prong,
Waiting for Mum to sing me that song!

Megan Darby (10)
Montpelier Junior School

FOOTBALL FEVER

F   ootball is the greatest,
O   h it is, by far,
O   h I wish I could go and watch a match,
T   ottenham versus Man U,
B   olton versus Sunderland,
A   fter the match, they go out till
L   ate at night, oh very
L   ate indeed.

Ben Ashurst (9)
Montpelier Junior School

MY FAVOURITE PLACE

Dartmoor is my favourite place,
Life is at a slow, slow pace.
Ponies, sheep and cattle roam,
Paths and tracks wind in the loam.
My pony I can ride all day,
Watching the animals as they lay.
I can cycle mile after mile,
Walking and climbing over the styles.
The mist comes down and hides the moon,
It's early now, upon Dartmoor.
The sun comes out again and shines,
Then darkness comes again,
To hide the beauty for that night,
Despite all this, there is no place
Quite as special as this space.

Andrew Ranson (11)
Plymouth College Preparatory School

NIGHT

Night is kind,
She is soft and warm.
She cares for you
And tucks you in at night.
Once and only once,
I saw that night was a lady,
A beautiful lady
Who rode across the fields
On a magnificent white horse.
I jump into bed,
I hear footsteps on the stairs,
Running, bang, bang, bang.
Her face as white as ice,
Her lips as red as a rose,
Then she sweeps her cloak over me and . . .
The kiss sends you into a deep sleep.
That's all I remember,
Till next time.

Ellie Jesty (11)
Plymouth College Preparatory School

REX

Rex the dog, who has huge teeth
And a nice furry underneath,
His hair is rough,
But he is quite tough.
He has a big nose
And eyes that glow.
He is Rex, the fantasy dog!

Adam Hext (10)
Plymouth College Preparatory School

NIGHT IS . . .

Night is a big, black panther,
Ready to pounce on you
To pin you to your bed,
So you can't get out.

The dark is a scary creature
Coming towards you.
You feel like just running away,
As far as possible.
Marooned on a volcanic island ready to erupt.

Night makes you think of werewolves and vampires.
I think night is a scary monster
Trying to get into my house.

His face is nasty and black, with
Glowing slits as eyes, like the moon,
And teeth as white as stars,
And black, wavy hair.

He wears black clothes.
He moves on a swift, black horse and
Does not live anywhere, he just floats
Around the world and makes me hide under my covers.

Cameron Thompson (10)
Plymouth College Preparatory School

LIFE

When the wind is high, leaves try to fly.
A river is like a mirror when it is still.
Planets look like eyes in the sky.
The hard hail tries to beat you down.

Trees try to grab with their branches,
Lightning flashing like a bulb that's just run out.
Owls' eyes glow in the dark.
Stones stay still as if they're petrified.

Freddie Martin (10)
Plymouth College Preparatory School

ORDERS OF THE DAY

Get up!
Eat your breakfast!
You are late!
Hurry up!
Into the car!
Get your book out!
Do not look at your lunch!
Hurry up, get into line!
Late for registration!
Go to English!
Get to work!
Aren't you ready!
Where have you been?
Look at your own work!
Stop mucking around!
Do not talk!
Eat your apple!
Do not spill your drink!
Shut up!
Go to sleep!
If we kids make such a fuss,
Why do you bother to keep
On having us?

Alexandra Wooler (9)
Plymouth College Preparatory School

OPINIONS OF ME

My baby cousin thinks I'm a 'super hero'
And that I ought to fly.

My grandma's made me her sole heir,
My brother doesn't know why.

Sonny believes I'm a cool dude
And the very best of men.

My girlfriend thinks I'm sexy,
She gives me eleven out of ten.

Mum tells me I'm her blue-eyed boy
And really quite a shopper.

Elliott thinks I'm a bighead
And gonna come a cropper.

Dad thinks I'm a nuisance,
But good upon a board.

Nan thinks I prance around,
Just like a lord.

Isaac Allen (10)
Plymouth College Preparatory School

NIGHT

Emerging from the deepest forest
To chase the sun around the world.

Night with his gaping mouth
That swallows all light around him,
And his long cloak that
Darkens the whole sky.

William Tyrrell-Moore (10)
Plymouth College Preparatory School

IN MY HEAD

In my head is an upside down world
With lots and lots of homework,
For doing away with French lessons.

And there is rugby, which shall come first.

And there is an entirely new tree,
An entirely new plane
And an entirely new car.

There is a dog that can live forever.

There is a multiplication table.

There is a chocolate world.

In my head is me and that's all that counts.

Tom Noble (11)
Plymouth College Preparatory School

MY GERBILS

Dart, hop, streak
Do the gerbils when they're free.
Off exploring my room,
Then scamper to nip me.
Sleek, velvet fur, beige, white and grey,
Tiny, sniffling in the hay.
Lettuce, carrot and apple too,
Chewing at their toy shoe.

Hannah Bolton (8)
Plymouth College Preparatory School

NIGHT

I find night quite nasty,
And very scary too.
He always makes me feel lonely,
He always gives me nightmares,
But sometimes, sweet dreams too.
When night comes to my house,
I tell him to go away,
But he always leaves my room
Saying, 'You will pay.'
He comes to my house the next night
With glowing eyes, so white.
When he comes in like that
He always gives me a fright.
His teeth are white with blood,
But his face is covered with a hood.
He moves swiftly through the air,
Giving me a right old scare.
I think he lives over the hill
With his friends I never see,
But all I know is,
He scares me.

Amy Pickard (10)
Plymouth College Preparatory School

THE SUNSET

As the sky turns pink
And the sun starts to sink,
The pot of gold melts into the field,
The cold, cold earth happy to yield.

When light and dark at last they met,
The trees are outlined in a silhouette.
The liquid creeping round every little bend,
This is a lovely way to see the day end.

Rachel Hughes (10)
Plymouth College Preparatory School

A CLOUD

A white, fluffy cloud,
Gliding through the sky.
Why it moves so slowly,
I'll never know why.

They disappear when it turns to night
And lose their colour of lovely, bright white.
Instead they turn a navy blue,
All the sky around them does too.

They will dance around all day
In a very pleasant way.
They will never, ever even stop,
Or make any noise, like an ear-splitting 'bang'
                              or a quite exciting 'pop'!

And when it turns to dawn,
A new day is reborn.
The sky turns pink and blue and reds
As people emerge from their warm, cosy beds.
The clouds will now emerge again
From their place in the sky,
Out of their comfy den.

Alice Bryant (9)
Plymouth College Preparatory School

ORDERS OF THE DAY

In my bedroom:

Wake up,
Pull the curtains,
Eat your breakfast,
Get dressed,
Tie your laces,
Turn off the TV,
Turn off the radio,
Close the door,
Take a shower,
Wash your face,
Brush your teeth,
Brush your hair.

I'm in school:

Stand straight,
You're late,
Be quiet,
Shhhhhh,
Get on,
Don't daydream,
Stop chatting,
Sit up straight,
Stop picking your nose,
Stop poking him,
Fold your arms,
Listen.

In the playground:

Don't do that,
Is that the a hometime ball?
I can get some rest.

Gabrielle Latifi (10)
Plymouth College Preparatory School

NIGHT

Night lives in a dark wood.
When it gets dark,
She comes and drags the darkness in.

She brushes with her frosty hands
The colours in the world
And paints the world black.

Her black twinkling eyes
Shimmer in the moonlight.
Her long black hair flows.

Her kind, frosty, sparkly face,
Her black lips,
Kiss daytime away.

When it comes to dawn,
Night is just a thing
Which lives in the wood.

Brogan Cusack (11)
Plymouth College Preparatory School

NIGHT

The night is like a wizard,
He casts spells into your mind.
His long black cloak is silent,
I feel him, safe and kind.

His spells make you fall asleep,
Your dreams drive fears away.
The wizard's wolf guards me through
And keeps bad dreams at bay.

You hardly hear him come,
He strides through right on time.
He creeps up on your shoulder
And peers into your mind.

His spells are from his staff,
They're lightning bolts of blue.
His horse is black, its hooves are grey,
While its silky mane blows in the wind down through.

Lawrence Robinson (10)
Plymouth College Preparatory School

DAY AND NIGHT

The sun blazes with happiness,
The wind whispers your name,
The clouds stroll along the sky,
The trees reach up to the sky,
As if trying to catch leaves.
A shooting star runs around the sky
As the moon glares down.
The sun says goodbye.

Vincent Markwood (11)
Plymouth College Preparatory School

HAPPY THURSDAY

Have a lovely day
And don't let things get you down.
Playing in a hockey match,
Playing with my dog,
Yellow leaves glinting in the sun,
Today is a very good day
For hopping and jumping around
Under the cool, wintry sun.
Remember to use up all your energy
So that you're all worn out.
Don't feel you need to rest,
Always do your best
And you'll come out on top.

Jessica Gates (10)
Plymouth College Preparatory School

SMUDGE, THE CAT

Smudge, the cat, is a jet-black and white cat.
Smudge, the cat, is a soft, smooth, sleek, black cat.
Smudge, the cat, moves quietly and carefully.
Smudge, the cat, can run very fast.
Smudge, the cat, can jump very high.
Smudge, the cat, curls up on the bed.
Smudge, the cat, catches mice, rabbits and birds.
He purrs when he's happy.
He's not loud or noisy.
When he's hungry he meows very quietly,
And he's my plain old Smudge.

William Dickinson (9)
Plymouth College Preparatory School

PLYMOUTH

Plymouth is a lovely city because it is by the sea.
Over two hundred thousand people live here, including me.
Parts of it, like the Barbican, are very, very old.
In the 17th century, the Pilgrim Fathers sailed from here to America,
                                                    I've been told.
Some of it is quite new, because during World War Two,
The city centre was badly bombed and had to be built anew.

There are a number of attractions here and plenty to see and do,
There's the Theatre Royal and the Pavilions with a fun pool
                                                    and ice rink too.
The Marine Aquarium in the Barbican is definitely worth a visit
                                                    in order to see
Many different fish, sharks, sea horses and other creatures
                                                    collected from the sea.
Plymouth Hoe is famous because Drake when playing bowls,
Spotted the Spanish Armada and was able to defeat them - to
                                                    their howls!

The view from Plymouth Hoe is rarely to be found,
Overlooking as it does the natural harbour of Plymouth Sound.
Lots of different boats come sailing in and out,
Naval ships, ferries, fishing boats and yachts quite safely, there
                                                    is no doubt.
Situated on the border of Devon and Cornwall and between the
                                                    moors and the sea,
It's a brilliant place to live, and many people think so, especially me!

Matthew Parven (10)
Plymouth College Preparatory School

THE ZOO

When I go to the zoo,
The first thing I do
Is watch the penguins eat.
They waddle around,
Without a sound,
On their spectacular feet!

Next I move on
And watch the lions roar.
They roar at me,
They roar some more,
Soon their throats will be sore!

After that, I see the monkeys
Gibbering nonsense at me.
I wish I could go in
And play with them,
But I don't have a key.

Then I go to the reptile house,
That's a fun thing to do.
Snakes' tails are so long,
It must be wrong.
Oh, I do like the zoo.

I see the seals, elephants and giraffe,
The parrots really make me laugh.
I do wish I had a bear for a pet,
This is a day I'll never forget!

Charlotte Wace (10)
Plymouth College Preparatory School

MY HOME

My home is a special place to me,
Where I always want to be.
I have a loving family waiting for me at home,
I have a cosy, cosy bed,
Where all my dreams come into my head.
My family feeds me every day,
But in my room I like to play,
I have a soft, cuddly cat,
Who lies down on a cuddly mat.
He miaows softly at night,
He gives me always a little fright.
I have the fish to feed every day,
I just lie there and watch them play.
My home will always be in my heart,
It always will play a special part.

Charlotte Bradfield (11)
Plymouth College Preparatory School

PEACE

Why can't we all be friends?
I long for a peace that never ends.
No bombs, no fighting, no killing,
We can do it, God willing.
Let everyone; white, brown, yellow and black,
Work together to keep us on a peaceful track.
Christians, Sikhs, Muslims and Hindu,
Together there is nothing we can't do.
United, we can conquer hunger, poverty and war
And live in harmony forever more.

Zoe Malone (8)
Plymouth College Preparatory School

STROLLING CLOUDS

The sun blazing down on the hot beach,
The clouds strolling along the sky.

The wind is whistling your name,
The sea running towards you like it's going to knock you over.

Then night comes back, it starts to rain,
Thunder and lightning, trees shout your name.

The moon gives that extra light,
Dogs run with fright.

It goes quiet.

Michael Hajiyianni (11)
Plymouth College Preparatory School

ANIMAL ANTICS

Seagulls swoop,
Elephants stomp,
Ducks whimper,
Frogs leap,
Foxes stalk,
Squirrels flitter,
Bees hover,
Lions pounce,
Hedgehogs crawl,
Jess bites,
Cats purr,
My brother fights,
Fish stir,
But I play.

Henry Littlewood (9)
Plymouth College Preparatory School

AUTUMN

Russet, rusty-gold,
The trees are looking old.
The grass is carpeted with leaves,
I'll have to roll up my sleeves.

The plants that are tall
Can almost reach over the wall.
The light from the lamp post shines on me,
Just before I climb the tree.

The ice-cold breeze
Is blowing around the leaves.
The only bird left
Is the robin and its nest.

Owen Binchy (9)
Plymouth College Preparatory School

THE COUNTRYSIDE

The sun is golden like a coin,
The clouds are walking along the pale blue sky.
The lake is clear, calm and still,
Fish are swimming, their scales like emptied stars.
The wind is whispering my name,
The birds are singing like a choir,
A mouse scuttles across the floor,
There is a frog perched on a lily pad, staring at me.
The trees are reaching up to the sky,
The leaves are flying around,
The grass is swaying, like a dance.

Louisha Meyrick (10)
Plymouth College Preparatory School

NATURE

The clouds, bleached a light orange colour by the sleepy sun,
Bound across the sky, as if to get away from the dim grey.
The trees glare at you in all the inky blackness.
The wind howls, whilst being murdered by the lightning bolts.
At dawn, the birds share all the gossip amongst the hedgerows.
A fox, guzzling down litres of water, looks into the river with
a mirror image.
Rabbits dart around in the early morning brightness.

George Greaves (10)
Plymouth College Preparatory School

THROUGH MY WINDOW

The wind is blowing,
The leaves are falling,
The trees are nearly bare,
But still a little bit of green
From all the evergreens.

No more lovely colours
Of flowers and fruits,
Now the colours are
Golden and brown.

Now the sun is going down,
The sky is pinky-red
And the day announces the night,
The only light is the moon.

Amy Meddings (9)
Plymouth College Preparatory School

DOLPHINS

Common, striped, bottlenose and many more,
Pacific, Atlantic, Indian and tropical islands, they adore.
Feeding on shrimps and crustaceans, the sea's natural resources,
Streamlined bodies, fins and flippers, of course.

Surfacing and diving in front of ships' bows,
Rolling and leaping, entertaining the crowds.
Film stars and documentaries, the leading part in all,
Highly intelligent, swimming in schools and having a ball.

Tragically hunted and killed by man,
Greenpeace and children, their number one fans,
But beware, the monster relation is near,
Orca, the killer whale, shows no fear.

So before venturing into the deep,
Be careful where you tread your feet!

Adele Crapnell (10)
Plymouth College Preparatory School

CAT

Grey and white and black,
Smooth fur,
It pounces,
It leaps,
It purrs,
It cleans its fur with its tongue,
It screeches,
It will kill mice, bats and pigeons.

Oliver May (8)
Plymouth College Preparatory School

THE MOON

The moon is a place in the sky.
The moon is a white splodge of ink
From a class in Heaven.
The moon is a ball stuck high in the sky.
The moon is a ball of string
That an old lady has for her knitting.
It is a cheesecake created by mice.
It is the cousin of the sun, the king of the night.
It is a roast potato feeding Heaven.
When the sun comes up, the moon sleeps,
Ready for the next night.
The moon is a bouncy castle
That spacemen jump on.
The moon is a light that is very bright
To help us see at night.
The moon is a saucer with milk filled to the top.
The moon is my friend.

Samuel Andrews (10)
Plymouth College Preparatory School

MY DOG

She sprints and bounces round and round,
She hardly ever touches the ground.
Her soft, smooth fur is very clean,
She's very fast, she's very keen.
She moves so gracefully in the air,
She goes almost everywhere, she does not care.
The way she barks is so, so loud,
I don't know, I think she's proud.

Oliver Wace (8)
Plymouth College Preparatory School

Snow Is ...

Snow is like a big, white sheet.
Snow is swans' feathers falling from the sky.
Snow is milk, frosted up.
Snow is like cotton wool laid upon the land.
Snow is Heaven, up very high.
Snow is clouds that have dropped on the ground.

Emma Gliddon (10)
Plymouth College Preparatory School

My Cat

My cat, she's dead now.
I can't remember when,
And I don't know how.
She was really old, (27 I think),
She was extremely black,
I really loved her lots and lots,
She'll never be forgot.

Matthew Smith (10)
Plymouth College Preparatory School

Conkers

C   onkers arrive at
O   ctober time,
N   ext to the tree they fall.
K   eep them in your pocket,
E   ven going to school.
R   ush into the playground,
S   mack them all.

Ralph Jones (9)
Plymouth College Preparatory School

CHOUGH

Jet-black,
Like a bat.

As coarse
As a carpet.

As fast
As a cat.

He bounds
Like a fox.

As sleek
As a wolf.

Ned Mumford (9)
Plymouth College Preparatory School

SNAKE SLIDE

It slithers,
It slides,
It hisses.
Some glide.
It's waterproof
In the rain.
I am thinking
About it
Again
And again.

Curtis Burchell (8)
Plymouth College Preparatory School

ANIMAL ANTICS

Seagulls peek,
Elephants stomp,
Ducks swim,
Frogs hop,
Foxes hide,
Squirrels scamper,
Bees buzz,
Lions roar,
Hedgehogs roll,
Birds glide,
Badgers hunt,
Snails slither,
Kangaroos jump,
I skip.

Mary Dashfield (8)
Plymouth College Preparatory School

OWL

Swooping around me,
High in the air,
His glare, his look, his stare.
He flies so quick and
Quietly in the air.
He stares at me
With his big, yellow eyes.
He swoops down
And I am gone.

Harry Leggett (10)
Plymouth College Preparatory School

SATURN'S RINGS

The rings of Saturn are golden bottle caps,
Thrown up into space.
Saturn's rings are yellow mists
Circling a giant, cream beach ball.
They are a halo around an angel's head.
They are shining, everlasting, multicoloured lights.
They are jewels from a pirate's treasure.

Guy Walker (10)
Plymouth College Preparatory School

FARMER

A farmer I want to be, to be,
When I grow up, just you see.
I'll milk the cows, shear the sheep,
Then back home to have a sleep.
Back to the fields we go with glee,
My cows, my sheep and me.

Danny Jenkins (10)
St Peter's RC Primary School

WINTER

W hen the wind begins to blow and the snow starts to fall,
I   watch it cover the ground gently.
N ice and warm inside, shivery outside.
T   onight I'm going to lie next to the fire, nice and warm.
E   verything outside is white,
R   acing around, throwing snowballs.

Adam Lee (9)
St Peter's RC Primary School

MY DREAMS

I go to bed to go to sleep,
The places I go,
The things I see
Are always a mystery,
A secret to keep.

Sometimes I'm a warrior,
A saviour, a hero.
Sometimes the victim,
Sometimes the villain,
But all the dreams have me in.

Last night I dreamt
I was running away
From some scary monster,
Covered in hay.

This morning I woke
And knew as I lay there
That it wasn't a monster,
Just my teddy bear!

Daniel Bresland (10)
St Peter's RC Primary School

WINTER'S HERE

Crackle goes the winter fire, warming our fingers and toes.
We are warm inside, but children are playing in the cold snow.
We invite them inside, from the cold winter's morn,
Then we watch snowflakes fall gently from the sky.
We sit down by the fire, marshmallows in hand,
We all sit staring at the snow-covered land.

Erin Tregunna (8)
St Peter's RC Primary School

COMPLAINT

The teachers all sit in the staffroom,
As cosy as can be,
And have a good view of the playground,
I don't know if they'll let you see.

We have to go out at playtime,
Unless we bring a note,
Or it's tipping down with rain,
Or we haven't got a coat.

We have to go out at playtime,
Whether we like it or not,
And freeze to death if it's freezing
And boil to death if it's hot.

The teachers all sit in the staffroom
And have a cosy chat.
We have to go out at playtime,
Where's the fairness in that?

Chris Smith (11)
St Peter's RC Primary School

CHILLY WEATHER

Chilly,
Frosty,
Bitter,
Snowy-blue icicles,
Snow-covered trees,
Frozen lakes,
Dismal hills,
Mountaintops glisten in the snow.

William Powell (8)
St Peter's RC Primary School

CHRISTMAS THOUGHTS

C arol singers singing softly,
H ungry robins on the fences,
R acing reindeer on the roof,
I cicles on the snowy trees.
S leepy children in their cosy beds,
T all Christmas trees with wrapped presents,
M usic playing very sweetly,
A ll stockings filled by Santa.
S tars shining brightly in the sky.

Sophie Payne (7)
St Peter's RC Primary School

CHRISTMAS

C hristmas was a lot of fun,
H appy faces on everyone,
R ipping open presents galore,
I 'd let anyone come in the door.
S tory books and Action Men,
T hen it's time for Mass at ten.
M ost of us have a giant plateful,
A nd for it all, we
S hould be grateful.

Katherine Rogers (10)
St Peter's RC Primary School

ANIMALS

Animals, animals, big and small,
Animals, animals, round and tall.
All the animals in Noah's ark,
Dogs that aren't allowed in parks.

Animals, animals, dogs and cats,
All the animals that like lots of pats.
All the animals that like to fly,
People are sad when animals die.

Amy Blades (9)
St Peter's RC Primary School

IT'S A SNOWY WINTER

It's a cold winter night,
Snow is drifting,
Skies are completely black.
Ice is crunchy,
Birds are really cold.
Children all in bed,
Gentle breeze blows around the
Cold, dark night.

Jamie Barnes (8)
St Peter's RC Primary School

THE OCEAN

The ocean is as blue as the sky.
Deep down in their homes,
The fish do not complain.
Shells still wash in and out.
The pebbles shine, the starfish glow,
But best of all, the corals grow.
The waves flow swiftly to the shore,
And the sea creatures like it more and more.

Jasmin Thompson (8)
St Peter's RC Primary School

MY LITTLE TABBY CAT

My little tabby cat, playful as can be,
Watching her chase her tail round and round.
My little tabby cat, playing with wool,
Oh, how she gets tangled in it!
My little tabby cat, off she goes,
Drifting into a cat sleep.
I wonder what she dreams?

Laura Mcleod (9)
St Peter's RC Primary School

SPRING

S   pring is the time when the hedgehogs, squirrels and birds
      wake up.
P   arks come alive with new growth.
R   abbits clean their burrows and prepare for new arrivals.
I   nsects begin to crawl around.
N   o more staying inside, lots of playing and running outside.
G   od is everywhere when it is spring.

Aoife Webb (7)
St Peter's RC Primary School

AUTUMN

A   s leaves fall gently to the ground,
U   mbrellas catching raindrops.
T   he wind takes them this way and that, like
U   nicorns jumping ropes.
M   e and my friends watch them drift,
N   ever stops until autumn is over.

Kathleen Chapman (8)
St Peter's RC Primary School

GRACE

Turning, twisting,
To-ing and fro-ing,
As graceful as a springbok's daughter.
Falling, rising,
Back and forthing,
Graceful as a swan in water.

Gentle, low, like nightingale's song,
Like the dew-covered grass that covers the lawn,
As it fills the air and echoes around,
The village is filled with this wonderful sound.

A song or a dance,
A nightingale's song,
The music or lyrics as I go along.
The sunlight that captures the new year's spring bulbs,
The horses in stables,
The lambs in their folds.

Madeleine Thomas (10)
St Peter's RC Primary School

CHRISTMAS

The sound of creaking on the stairs,
The bells are sweetly ringing.
Brightly wrapped toys,
Waiting for tomorrow,
Holly, spiky leaves
And berries hanging.
Scented candles fill the air.
Pudding, mince pies, crackers,
All make Christmas.

Ashlea James (8)
St Peter's RC Primary School

AUTUMN

Autumn leaves are falling
Softly in the wind,
Crimson, gold,
Creamy green,
Lovely patchwork quilts under every tree.

I love to see the trees,
Yes, oh those ballerinas falling in the breeze.
Summer is good,
However, autumn is the best,
So watch out for those falling leaves.

Rachel Sturgeon (9)
St Peter's RC Primary School

NIGHT

In the darkness, in the gloom,
The stars are shining and the moon.
The cool wind is blowing,
The sharp lamps are glowing.
The people are walking to look into the sky
And watch the stars go by.

The children are sleeping,
The adults are creeping.
The lonely street,
The dark night to keep.

Kelly Wheeler (10)
St Peter's RC Primary School

AUTUMN

Girls and boys play on the leaves,
Crunch, crunch, crunch.

The clouds are heavy in the sky,
Rain, rain, rain.

Squirrels collecting food,
Nuts, nuts, nuts.

Leaves turn beautiful colours,
Red, orange, yellow.

Harriet Oliver (8)
St Peter's RC Primary School

STORMS

My mum hates thunder,
She plugs her ears with a towel
And lies on the settee,
As though someone was coming to get her.

But me, I'm all right,
I don't mind a bit.
I'm a big edgy about lightning,
But thunder doesn't bother me at all.

Cameron Meakin (8)
St Peter's RC Primary School

CATS

Cats leaping,
Pouncing on mice,
Bushy tails up in the air,
Running like the wind,
Hiding in bushes.

Playing with their toys,
Pawing their balls,
Chasing a piece of string,
Playing with spiders,
Running down the stairs.

Sitting by the fire,
Lying down and purring,
Snuggled up in bedclothes,
Peacefully sleeping,
Dreaming of a clockwork mouse.

Charlotte Buller (10)
St Peter's RC Primary School

BACK TO SCHOOL

Why do we have to go back to school?
The holidays have been so cool!
I wish we had just one day more,
Before teachers again begin to bore.

A holiday which lasts all year,
A break to get our brains in gear!
Roll on every weekend, I wish they came each day,
Come on, they're just around the bend,
Roll on Saturday!

Katie Hawke (10)
St Peter's RC Primary School

MYSELF

S ooty is my cat.
O melettes I eat.
P eter is my grandad.
H enry is my dog.
I zzy is my best friend.
E aster eggs I like.

A nn is my middle name.
N umber work I find easy.
N o one is the same as me.

B arbecues I enjoy.
U nderneath my feet I feel the ground.
L ouise is my little cousin.
L emon meringue pie is delicious.
E eyore is my favourite Winnie the Pooh character.
R oast dinner is scrummy.

Sophie Ann Buller, that's my name.

Sophie Buller (8)
St Peter's RC Primary School

AUTUMN

Grey clouds are gathering
Like hungry seagulls.
Burnt orange, sunset-red,
Hot yellow and mint green.
Flash and swirl like
Acrobats in a blustery wind.
They tumble and fall,
Covering the ground
Like a multicoloured carpet.

Johnny Jenkins (8)
St Peter's RC Primary School

MY ALIEN CAT

My cat watches me from the corner of her eye and purrs.
My cat is blue and green with pink spots and horns, is yours?
My cat can talk and breathe fire too.
My cat can sing a lullaby to me or to you,
And drive a car, a motorbike, a plane and even a spaceship.
My cat does her multiplication.
My cat can do my homework as well.
My cat plays the keyboard, guitar and clarinet.
She plays football better then Owen and Beckham or you!
My cat can swim eighty-six lengths of the pool,
Take over the world, or take over you.
My cat can do whatever she likes,
So next time you see a cat
Sitting on the wall,
Just wonder, just wonder!

Holly Malek (9)
St Peter's RC Primary School

CHRISTMAS

C hristmas is a celebration time,
H appy children play in the snow.
R ustling of wrapping paper,
I   ndigo, gold and red.
S anta is coming on his sleigh.
T urkey, stuffing, nuts and sweets.
M um and Dad exchanging presents,
A ll the family singing happily.
S now is still falling heavily.

James Paskins (8)
St Peter's RC Primary School

JAGUARS

Jaguars are big,
Jaguars are strong,
They like meat
And can run.
Their eyes like sapphires
Glow at night,
Cold, but colourful,
They sleep tight.

Harry Morse (8)
St Peter's RC Primary School

PLEASURE TREASURE

Down to the bottom of the sea I go,
In search of hidden treasure.
Battling against the water's flow,
Do I really do this for pleasure?

Down to the bottom of the sea I go,
In search of pearls and gold.
Why do I do this? I don't know,
I think I am getting too old.

Down to the bottom of the sea I go,
And finally find my treasure.
It's not pearls and gold though,
It's diving for pleasure!

Ami Price-Draper (10)
Wembury CP School

MY TREASURE!

Under the deep, dark, blue sea,
Hidden is the golden treasure key.
To get it, you have to look and look,
If you get there last, it was probably took.

You have to read books and look at maps,
Also you have to wear an oxygen mask with difficult straps.
On my back is an oxygen tank,
It helps me dive to where the ship sank.

Deep, deep, down I go,
As I get closer, I see the treasure glow,
But where is the golden key I cannot find?
There it is, the key that sparkles and shines.

As I dive down to the treasure,
It gives me most, great pleasure.
As I go to put the key in,
I have just had a big win!

I have found the treasure.

Sophie Byrne (10)
Wembury CP School

OH NO, NOT AGAIN!

I had a little accident,
A cut, my thumb, oh the pain!
'Off to casualty,' said Dad.
Oh no, not again!

I had a little accident,
I fell, my toes, oh the pain!
'A trip to casualty,' said Mum.
Oh no, not again!

I had a little accident,
I fell, my ankle, oh the pain!
'Off to casualty,' said Mum and Dad.
Oh no, not again!

'Broken ankle,' said the doctor,
'Not a sprain!'
He looked up at me and cried,
'Oh no, not again!'

Larissa Toms (11)
Wembury CP School

TREASURE ADVENTURE

There was a girl called Heather
And she wanted to find some treasure,
So she got an air tank,
And she put her swimsuit on, but she was nearly bare.
When she got to the beach,
Heather jumped up and landed in the sea.

Heather swam deep down into the sea,
Later on she saw some gold.
She swam near to have a look,
But it was only a lump of sand, so she swam away.

She swam further on,
Heather saw another piece of gold,
But it was only a nice shell.
So she swam away again.

Soon she came to a big chest, she swam closer
And there was a huge amount of gold in it.
Then she took some gold and a beautiful diamond necklace
And swam happily home.

Anna Hunt (9)
Wembury CP School

MY SISTER

She ripped up my homework,
She stole my notepad,
She locked me in the toilet
And told me I was sad.

When we walked to school,
She ran ahead of me.
She looked at me and laughed
With a smiling face of glee.

At school she'd pretend she didn't know me,
She'd run away if I came near.
She'd smile at her friends, but not at me
And she told all the teachers that I was queer.

But one day she totally changed,
She helped me with my homework,
She gave me back my notepad
And she didn't lurk,
Because . . .

She had found a little something,
Called a hidden treasure.
I hope she carries on like this
Because what my sister had found was
Pleasure!

Olivia Horton (11)
Wembury CP School

THE TREASURES AT MY SCHOOL

My hidden treasure is my school,
Oh, and not forgetting the swimming pool.
It means a lot to me
And sometimes I get upset when I go home for my tea!
I especially enjoy maths
And also stepping along the literacy path.
I'll soon be at my secondary school,
There, I'll miss my present school,
But the things I'll miss most are the teachers and my mates,
The people who you can say to, 'Oh, hang on a minute,'
And there they'll stand and wait.
Then you've got the brainies,
Who give you a quiz when it's rainy.
Oh and not forgetting the cleverest of them all,
That when you look up at them they stand all lean and tall.
Do you know who I'm talking about?
They are the best without a doubt.
You guessed, it's the teachers!

So next time you to go to school,
Think, is it your hidden treasure?
Because I know one thing that is certain,
My hidden treasure is my school!

Rebecca Davies (10)
Wembury CP School

MY LITTLE SISTER

That's my little sister,
Just two weeks old.

I cannot call her 'sister',
Therefore, what shall she be called?

I want to call her Daisy,
But daisies are flowers.

I want to call her 'stupid',
But she would punch me on the nose.

I want to call her nightingale,
But she does not sound like a bird.

The doctor called her pretty,
But pretty's not the word.

The nurse called her 'beauty',
But Beauty is a horse.

We do not have a name,
But we are so glad she's here.

There's one thing I will not forget,
That my little sister is my hidden treasure.

Katie Finch (10)
Wembury CP School

THE ARCTIC RABBIT

A glitter of snowflake,
Sparkles on the ice,
The rabbit runs,
A streak of white.

Ben Wheatley (9)
Widey Court Primary School

IN THE ARCTIC

As cold as frost,
The rivers aren't rivers,
They're as cold as ice,
Not a piece of sun.

As cold as frost,
You think it's all right,
You dare climb a mountain,
It's kind of frightening.

A dream of midnight,
Getting back,
But it's just snow.

A ball of fire,
That's all we dream
And he's left, stuck there.

Michael Heape (9)
Widey Court Primary School

WINTER DAYS

A mist of cold wind,
A touch of icy breath,
A breeze of snow,
A river of white ice.

A sparkle of snowflakes,
A silent world,
A dark night,
A diamond light.

Ben Harkin (10)
Widey Court Primary School

A MISTY LAND

No sound at all,
A land of ice,
Soft movements,
A shower of ice.

Mist all over,
Hard to see,
Something watching,
Twinkling and glistening.

Something moving,
White as snow,
Very soft movements,
It's like angels gliding by.

The land goes quiet,
Who knows why?
Something watching from the sky.

The sun comes up,
The moon goes down,
But the mist is still there.

Tianna Halling (10)
Widey Court Primary School

THE CAT

The cat is quick, the cat is sly,
The snow beds are high, the cat is low,
He's going to pounce into a lot of snow
Because there is a snail that's oh so slow.
The heather is rising, the cat is going,
As quick as it came, it was go, go, going.

Kirk Sturrock (10)
Widey Court Primary School

WINTER

A mist of wind,
A touch of breath,
A ruby of love,
A shiver of cold.

A sparkle of snowflake,
A mist of fog,
A touch of frost,
A ball of fire.

A lake of ice,
A diamond of light,
A crystal of silence,
Winter is here.

Elliott Key (9)
Widey Court Primary School

ICY THOUGHTS

A starlight of gold,
An angel of cold,
A shiver of feathers,
The white dream.

Wind that whirls,
Some diamonds like pearls,
No sound at all,
Not even a whisper.

The snowflake of glitter,
Like icing, but cold,
A fantasy of snow.

Selina Boundy (10)
Widey Court Primary School

IN THE COLD

A glimpse of sunlight
From a hot, summer day,
When the sun passes over the moon,
That's empty as moonlight.

Nothing around,
Not even a topaz of rain.
See a strong light
That's full of flames.

There was a crystal of silence,
A snowflake of feathers
And something around,
Like an island of paradise.

I walked a little further,
I froze in the cold,
I stood still - and I shivered!

Kiah Rosenstein (10)
Widey Court Primary School

ICY CRYSTALS

A diamond of light,
A feather of ice,
A shiver of cold,
A ruby of love,
A land of stillness,
An island of paradise,
A twinkle of snow,
A sparkling crystal.

Kori Hooper (9)
Widey Court Primary School

A World Of Ice

Camouflaged in a world of ice,
No one to see him,
No one to fight.

Hungrily digging through the ice,
No seal to see,
Desperate for food.

At last, a faint smell.
Digging, digging fast,
But the seal escapes!

She is lucky,
But the polar bear
Will strike again!

Keeley Quintrell (9)
Widey Court Primary School

What Does It Mean?

A lake of ice,
What does that mean?
A touch of frost,
What does that mean?
A sparkle of a snowflake,
What does that mean?
A crystal of silence,
What does that mean?

Winter is here!

Jade Cox (10)
Widey Court Primary School

THE ARCTIC RABBIT

Standing motionless,
A rustle of fur
As the wind blows.

It waits patiently,
A breath of ice,
A touch of chill.

An emerald of snow,
The blue moon shines,
A blue streak like the sea.

A pink light fills the sky,
Dawn is nearby,
But it can't find what the moon found.

It is amongst the snow.
It's there, but no one knows,
But it's there.

Megan McCarthy (10)
Widey Court Primary School

THE ARCTIC SEAL

No river, just ice,
Island of paradise.
A dream of wonders,
A forest of snow.

Nothing moving,
Not even a flake,
Only a leaf on
The puddle, it flows.

A twinkle of frost,
A touch of ice,
Poor little seal,
Nothing to eat.

Victoria Bolton (9)
Widey Court Primary School

A WHITE DREAM

No sound at all,
A world of ice,
An empty place,
A twinkle of light.

The North Star,
A mountain of heather,
A cramped place,
A shiver of cold.

A frozen world,
A snowball of shiver,
A land of quietness,
A flow of wind.

Something is moving,
But what could it be?
A star of glitter.

The moon is rising,
The sun has gone,
A sparkle of light.

Tanya Hedges (9)
Widey Court Primary School

IN A LAND OF SNOW

Camouflaged in a land of snow,
He wants to catch something,
But he'll have to stay low.
In a whirling blizzard he stalks his prey,
Ready to pounce at the slightest move.
He'll never give up, he has to stay,
Then he sees something move in the river of frost.
He dives on the ice, waiting near a hole,
It surfaces, sniffing around. He misses.
The seal swims off, but the polar bear is left there . . .
Waiting, waiting, waiting.

Sarah Vellacott (10)
Widey Court Primary School

A MIDNIGHT DREAM

No sound at all,
As white as ice,
The glitter of a star
Is in the cold.

Nowhere in sight,
There was a sound,
A midnight dream
Is in the air.

In the freezing cold,
A starlight of whiteness
Is a midnight dream.

Laura Chilvers (9)
Widey Court Primary School

A MYSTERY ANIMAL

A roar of a lion
And a punch of a boxer,
A bite of a tiger
And a scratch of a panther.

The swim of a dog,
The pounce of a cat,
The speed of a leopard,
But he's not a cat.

He sees the lake, he waits and waits,
He sees the seal that he truly hates.
He pounces, he misses,
He walks away,
But some day, some day,
The polar bear will catch the seal,
For he cannot be seen on the snow.

Samuel Daniels (10)
Widey Court Primary School

THE ARCTIC RABBIT

Running through the Arctic,
Like a snowflake of crystal,
He'll be camouflaged by the snow,
Until the big bear is hungry.

He'll run like nothing you've seen before,
He won't give up until he finds his way home.
When he stops, it'll be like a dream of sparkles.

Adam Winsor (10)
Widey Court Primary School

SILENCE

It was so silent that I heard
The clouds swaying,
Like the deep, blue ocean.

It was so peaceful that I heard
The wind whispering to me,
Like leaves rustling from miles away.

It was so restful that I heard
Pages of books swinging from side to side,
Like pencils tapping on desks, harshly.

Hayley Starkey (10)
Widey Court Primary School

SNAKE

Rat hunter,
Egg taker,
Venomous biter,
Body binder,
Prey stalker.
Air taster,
Tail rattler,
Slow swallower,
Smooth slitherer.

A recipe to make
. . . a snake.

Daniel Clancy & Samuel Cogley (11)
Woodfield Primary School

DOLPHIN

Fish gobbler,
Shark killer,
Pack hunter.

Air breather,
Strong swimmer,
Deep thinker.

People lover,
Great entertainer,
Water dancer.

A bottle-nosed dolphin.

Terry Carter & Danny Nicholls (11)
Woodfield Primary School

A SHARK!

Whale attacker,
Dolphin biter,
Fish swallower,
Boat destroyer.

Baby carer,
Sleek swimmer,
Long looker,
Steady hunter.

A white shark!

Rebecca Sheikh & Shannon Harte (10)
Woodfield Primary School

A DOG

Aggressive player,
Cat chaser,
Animal teaser,
Postman biter.

Bone gnawer,
Toy fetcher,
Noisy drinker,
Grass roller.

Rapid runner,
Deafening barker,
Dream sleeper,
Body scratcher.

Hedge hider,
Scent sniffer.

Ellen Miller, Chloe Dodd (10)
*   & Lucy Edney (11)*
Woodfield Primary School

CATS

Mouse catcher,
Mad scratcher,
Milk sipper,
Food nipper,
Silent sleeper,
Leg stretcher,
Sneaky strutter,
Wall springer,
Toy player.

Matthew Parker (11) & Adam Prout (10)
Woodfield Primary School

CLEANER

Gentle sweeper,
Brilliant duster,
Floor mopper,
Table polisher.

Carpet hooverer,
Window washer,
Door locker,
Toilet cleaner.

Cloth carrier,
Bucket swiller,
Overall wearer,
Wonderful worker.

Kyle Prior & Chris Miller (10)
Woodfield Primary School

BEAR

Tree climber,
Honey finder,
Perfect hunter,
River punter,
Cub carer,
Skin tearer,
Heavy sleeper,
Crafty creeper,
Fish cruncher,
Berry muncher.

Ross Hellyer, Ryan Hansford (10)
*   & Jordan Boulter (11)*
Woodfield Primary School

TEENAGER

Fashion-follower,
Jewellery-wearer,
Bedroom-lover,
Computer-player.

Wailing-whinger,
Mood-swinger,
Serious-stropper,
Arm-flopper.

Music-blarer,
Telly-hogger,
Back-chatter,
Zit-zapper.

A recipe to make a
Teenager.

Rhys Riley & Jordan Isaacs (10)
Woodfield Primary School

POLICEMAN

Street plodder,
Speedy driver,
Crime stopper,
Thief taker.

Gifted communicator,
Court talker,
Community carer,
Lost child finder.

Christopher Holland, Leah Lowe (11)
                    & Gareth Fice (10)
Woodfield Primary School

TAXI DRIVER

People carrier,
Coffee drinker,
Money collector,
Night driver.

Microphone speaker,
Sandwich eater,
Map reader,
Petrol filler.

Chris Pickering (11), Bret Widdicombe
*   & Stacey Cutting (10)*
Woodfield Primary School

DOG

Fierce-biter,
Lively-barker.

Cat-hater,
Tail-chaser.

Meat-gobbler,
Scent-sniffer.

A recipe to make
A dog.

Jessica Cutler (11) & Stephannie Cooksley (10)
Woodfield Primary School